O'Neil Ford Duograph 3: Argentina

Altamira Building, 1998–2001
Rafael Iglesia

Florencia Raigal House, 2005–2006
Marcelo Villafañe

The O'Neil Ford Duograph Series, Volume 3
– Argentina
Altamira Building, Florencia Raigal House
THE UNIVERSITY OF TEXAS AT AUSTIN
Center for American Architecture and Design
O'Neil Ford Chair in Architecture

Editor
Wilfried Wang

Essays
Rafael Iglesia
Federico Pastorino
Juan Manuel Rois
Marcelo Villafañe
Wilfried Wang

Series Editors
Kevin Alter
Michael Benedikt
Barbara Hoidn
Wilfried Wang

Associate Editors
Daniel Sylvester
Barbara Terrell

Production Editors
Susan McNally
Christine Wong

Design
Daniel Sylvester

Printed and bound in Canada.

Sole Distributor in Europe:
Ernst Wasmuth Verlag GmbH & Co.
Fürststrasse 133
72072 Tübingen, Germany
www.wasmuth-verlag.de
info@wasmuth-verlag.de

ISBN 978-3-8030-0719-3

Sole Distributor in the United States of America and Canada:
D.A.P. / Distributed Art Publishers
155 Sixth Avenue, 2nd Floor
New York, New York 10013, U.S.A.
Tel. (212) 627-1999, Fax. (212) 627-9484

Contents

O'NFM 3

Foreward

Rosario

Wilfried Wang

With this third volume in the *O'Neil Ford Duograph* series, the Center for American Architecture and Design (CAAD) and the O'Neil Ford Chair in Architecture at The University of Texas at Austin continue to present contributions significant in breadth and depth to contemporary architecture. Following our presentation of Chiléan and Brazilian architects in volume 2, we continue the series with two more architects from a South American country, this time Argentina. While the two selected architects would never claim to represent the nation, in a curious way, the two building types are indicative of the "typical" commissions there: high-rises for the downtown areas and villas for the suburbs. Each building type has, of course, excelled in history with numerous exemplary cases; for this reason, the selection of one more high-rise and yet another house for a publication is quite rightly to be met with strong dose of skepticism.

Are the two buildings chosen for this issue of the *O'Neil Ford Duograph* really significantly different from, say, the bulk of Argentinian or South American or indeed global production? While the editors' answers are a foregone conclusion, the readers are invited to judge for themselves. What is so special about a slim, reinforced concrete, high-rise building in a downtown area of a South American city? What is so unique about a small, free-standing house, right in the middle of the Pampas? Seeing it from a distance, one must surely answer "nothing."

The privilege of traveling to these places opens another perspective onto these buildings and many others by contemporary architects in South America. Seeing the buildings in their contexts and in their material reality casts an entirely different light on them. Probing the structures, walking through them, seeing them in use, all of this allows another reading. Both buildings presented in this issue are "true normal types" as Louis Sullivan defined the term. It would be possible to go further: they are both radically normal. Their normality is achieved by their material constituency: reinforced concrete and concrete blocks respectively. Indeed, none of the materials are at all special. But then, these materials are disposed uniquely: both flex their spaces and create tensely productive relations between interior and exterior. In the context of contemporary architecture, their languages are not particularly "special"; what makes each special is their integrity of concept, program, structure, spatial formation and material realization. It is in this sense that the two buildings are significant and yet also exemplary of a radical normality.

Seen from a distance, these two buildings may be valued in the international context. With the advantage of information technology such as the conventional professional journals and the more novel internet, projects of all intentions, shapes and sizes are brought to any interested and probing person's attention. Many observers have experienced the difference between initial curiosity for some seemingly unusual building and subsequent denouement, or revelation, upon closer examination. What may have looked irresistable from afar, often turns out to be far from agreeable.

Rafel Iglesia, born 1952 in Concordia (Entre Ríos, Argentina), and Marcelo Villafañe, born 1951 in Rosario (Santa Fe, Argentina), are part of a intense community of architects, "Groupo R." Next to the two larger cities of Buenos Aires and Córdoba, Rosario constitutes an experimental laboratory for small-to-medium scale architecture, a scale that favors middle class clients and developers. Compared with the northern hemisphere, building costs are low while the complete range of construction trades is available. Although one would not claim the level of execution to be of any higher quality than in any other post-industrialized region, the role and authority of the architect is somewhat more elevated here than in more so-called developed countries. This has given both of the architects presented in this duograph the opportunity to carry out their individual personal research programs—in both cases involving the use of wood as a the base material (in their earlier projects)—so as to carry these programs forward in more complex conceptions for later commissions.

Iglesia's cantilevering staircase (Rosario, 2001) and Villafañe's plywood sunshade and sliding screen (Rosario, 1996) are miniature manifestos, each foreshadowing their potential as full scale architectural ideas. On the one hand, such a progression may be regarded in retrospect as being fortunate, some observers might even dismiss such an approach as being obsessively myopic. On the other hand, it demonstrates to those believing in the power of architectural concepts and potentials, regardless of the scale of realization, that the perspicacity for the essential distinguishes those architects interested in the core of architectural discipline from those who are more endeared to either word games or shape-making for its own sake.

One common inspiration for both Iglesia and Villafañe is the work of José Enrique Scrimaglio, born 1937 in Rosario. His masterfully disciplined pieces, mostly constructed in brick, can be situated between the late works of Frank Lloyd Wright, Louis Kahn, Sigurd Lewerentz, and Heinz Bienefeld. Scrimaglio's spiritual and intellectual intensity has certainly projected itself on the thinking of both Iglesia and Villafañe. However, even more so has Scrimaglio's sheer enjoyment in the correct placement of one brick against another inspired many younger architects. This embrace of fundamental architectural rigor has laid a common, if unspoken, foundation for so many Rosario architects.

A third colleague, not represented in this duograph, but to be included in the CAAD publication *CENTER: Latitudes, Architecture in the Americas*, following the 2009 and 2010 *Latitudes Conferences* at the University of Texas at Austin School of Architecture, is Gerardo Caballero, born 1957 in Totoras (Santa Fe, Argentina). Caballero's work has been influenced by his reading of conventional, anonymous agricultural buildings of the Pampas. Equally, the liberating nonchalance of lessons learned from early works by from Robert Venturi allowed Caballero to create spatial complexities that are projected into the public domain by large, almost billboard-like openings (e.g., the stores for agricultural equipment on Ruta 34 of 2007, for bicycles in Rosario of 2009, or the Casa Puerto Roldan in Roldan of 2007). Since 2008, Caballero has been the architect of the urban development and architecture of the former Puerto Norte warehouse district, the largest single development in Rosario in the first decade of the 21st century.

Rosario, nearly two hundred miles northwest of Buenos Aires, is situated on the Paraná River. A city of about 1.2 million inhabitants with a narrow, downtown street grid based on the colonial layout, it is now occupied with numerous high-rises and some remnants of a grander architectural era, including the National Flag Memorial of 1957 by Àngel Guido and Alejandro Bustillo, which commemorates General Manuel Belgrano, creator of the Argentinian flag. Most notable is the city's recent successful implementation of a continuous embankment park along the Paraná River, a phased project in which Caballero (segment of the Paseo del Caminante of 1996–67) and Villafañe (Parque de las Colectividades of 2006 and the project for the MACRO museum of 2009) have been directly involved.

To visitors interested in architecture there is the sense that an intense network of architects is emerging from the small scale of building production to gradually influence the city's urban and architectural development. This duograph is a tribute to two of them, who are representative of the larger Rosario network.

Altamira Building, 1998 – 2001
Rafael Iglesia

Essay

Altamira

Wilfried Wang

The classical column is the enduring and seemingly inescapable formal reference for high rise designs. In his essay "The Tall Office Building Artistically Considered," Louis Sullivan refers to this orthodox conception: "the true prototype of the tall office building is the classical column, consisting of base, shaft and capital."[1] For architects designing any high-rise building, the column may indeed be the prototype. For the general public, the classical column could be claimed to be more than that, namely, the archetype. Struggling against this archetype throughout his career, Sullivan was searching for the high-rise's contemporary equivalent of the fitness-to-function, as seen in the Greek temple, the Gothic cathedral or the medieval fortress. In the same essay, Sullivan emphatically pronounces that "form ever follows function. This is the law." Thus Sullivan, while acknowledging the tripartite division of any high-rise's functions (the lower one or two stories for special needs, followed by repetitive offices and topped by a conclusive attic), rejected the design of high-rises based on proto- or archetypes, calling instead for a natural, spontaneous and unwitting conclusiveness to a building's innermost functions, in short, "a true normal type."[2]

Although the special needs of the lower two floors may indeed be co-determined by the high-rise's interior needs, there are other expectations that architecture needs to satisfy. There is firstly the high-rise's outward manifestation, its shape, and secondly its node-like quality of interfacing with the surrounding urban silhouette—two issues that seem to be tautologically related, but in fact address distinct orders of cognition. On the issue of its outward manifestation, any building possesses a configurational character beyond the simple assembly of spaces, structural systems or constructional layers; any building has a shape or *gestalt*, be it a simple box or a metaphor with reference to some other object.

Whereas the literal classical column, as proposed by Adolf Loos in his entry to the Chicago Tribune Tower competition in 1922, was too obvious an embodiment of the expected archetype, clearly the quasi neo-plasticist proposal with the decorative horizontal fins for the same competition by Walter Gropius and Adolf Meyer could not command the respect of the client organization either. Nonetheless, despite a range of pioneering designs, the realized tower by Raymond Hood and John Mead Howell with all its academic neo-Gothic elements, does represent a true normal type in the sense in which the clients and no doubt the largest part of the general public were expecting the tower to appear. The realized Chicago Tribune Tower brings together a logical and conventional circulation core with a minimal structure of eight internal pillars in an otherwise open plan. The neo-Gothic pillars, soaring like the Gothic cathedrals, are indeed exo-skeletal load-bearing elements. The projecting central bays and the chamfered corners of the plan allow the shaft of the tower to approximate to a circle, and thus the visual effect of the Neo-Gothic abutments in combination with the recessed windows constitute a modulation of the configuration not unlike the fluting of a Doric column. Hood and Howell's design thus successfully modulates the tectonic and configurational elements of the Chicago Tribune Tower so as to maximize flexibility of the floor plate and minimize structural components while integrating the configurational elements in such a way as to create a depth and complexity of the external surface that underscores the tower's verticality.

However, while Adolf Loos' literally enlarged Chicago Tribune Column would have required a more complex geometry and, given the entasis of the shaft, in turn a more complicated structural system, Hood and Howell's design represents a

1. Louis H. Sullivan, "The Tall Office Building Artistically Considered," *Lippincott's Magazine*, vol. 57, Philadelphia, March 1896, pp. 403-9.

2. *ibid.*, "the tall office building should not, must not, be made a held for the display of architectural knowledge in the encyclopedic sense; that too much learning in this instance is fully as dangerous, as obnoxious, as too little learning; that miscellany is abhorrent to their sense."

more rational and more easily buildable structure of greater delicacy. These considerations are raised to emphasize the fact that numerous morphological parallels exist between Loos' literal column and the realized building, and that the development of "a true normal type" was only to be undertaken over two decades later by Ludwig Mies van der Rohe—specifically in the application of the projecting I-beam mullions. These would give the high-rises, such as at 860–880 Lake Shore Drive of 1949, an abstracted form of fluting. In this instance, the variegated colors in the façade would diminish the vertical effect of the mullions, a loss that was overcome by the use of dark bronze in the case of the Seagram Building of 1958. The force of the vertical member translated into the principle of fluting, in both the Chicago Tribune Tower and the Seagram Building, is thus a persistent formal legacy that helped to establish the first normal type for a high-rise.

The logic of the three-dimensional skeletal frame with applied facade panels had thus run its course. Subsequent high-rises would be more or less intelligent variations on this theme. With the disappearance of the "Miesian corner," the vestigial evidence of the tall building's structural logic, behind a continuous envelope—all around and from top to bottom—the architects' interest increasingly shifted to the design of the skin and the building's shape as a relatively autonomous concern. Such an uncoupling from both the archetype—the Doric column—and the Miesian abstracted instance would lead to a post-modernist festival on the one hand and a free form free-for-all on the other. High-rise conceptions since then have been as varied as human imagination has permitted. The critique of skyscraper design during the last decade of the 20th-century took note of this decadent design attitude.

Sullivan's ideal of a logical relation between function and form has had to wait a few decades after the Seagram Building to see integral research into high-rise design. To be sure, the hyper-structural concerns of Louis Kahn and Anne Tyng, as seen in their Municipal Offices in Philadelphia (1952–57, influenced by Buckminster Fuller's geometric and structural research) and Kisho Kurokawa's Helix City (1961) and Kenzo Tange with his Tokyo Bay project (1964) would logically lead to such tall structures as the John Hancock Tower in Chicago (1965–69) by Fazlur Khan of SOM, the National Bank of Jeddah (1983) also by SOM, and a typological precursor to the Commerzbank Tower in Frankfurt am Main (1993–97) by Foster + Partners. The latter two high-rises indeed proved to be pioneers in conceiving tall buildings not as a continuous vertical extrusion of repetitive slabs, albeit tapered to conform to basic structural requirements, but as consisting of meta-configurational components that would be stacked either in a diminishing helical-pyramidal order or as a quasi-woven fabric on a giant scale.

With all of these high-rise permutations one particular design dilemma has persisted: to which extent should the constituting elements of a large structure be visually present and distinct, and to which extent should the overall form be predominant? Such a general dilemma of the relationship of the part to the whole exists at all levels of architectural design, and it is in the architect's domain that the complexities of each dimension's representational needs are resolved. Given the exposed conditions of many high-rises, this dilemma comes to the fore in such designs. The high-rise's gestalt might, after all, also allow the interested observer to deduce the structural and constructional logics of the building.

With Rafael Iglesia's Altamira, a compositional and structural logic has been reinterpreted to generate a tall building that is as direct as a house of cards—finally a coherent neo-plasticist structure that embodies an inner discipline so lacking in the original neo-plasticism of Theo van Doesburg and Cornelis van Eesteren. Their

Contra-Construction of 1923, itself an attempt at inverting traditional structural logic, was an implied three-dimensional, compositional version of Piet Mondrian's picturesque, black grid-bound color fields; its promise of utter compositional freedom, albeit corseted within an orthogonal geometry, has survived as an idea in compositions of countless buildings, from simple houses to large commercial structures. Iglesia's Altamira high-rise is fundamentally different, even though the atmosphere of neo-plasticism's compositional freedom lingers here. Altamira's structural system can be read twofold: as a helical set of connected concrete walls and beams and as a vertically stacking set of slabs.

The former reading of the structural system is underlined by the composition of the walls and beams facing the street. The temptingly minimal connections between the tectonic elements emphasize the rotational flow of forces. The control exerted over the concentration of vertical circulation elements and services in the depth of the site, as far away as possible from the street, frees the cantilevering loft-like spaces facing the public to celebrate lightness and daring. A selective staircase system divides the high-rise into two different units: on the one hand, just a loft and, on the other hand, an apartment with two bedrooms off the core. In the latter case,

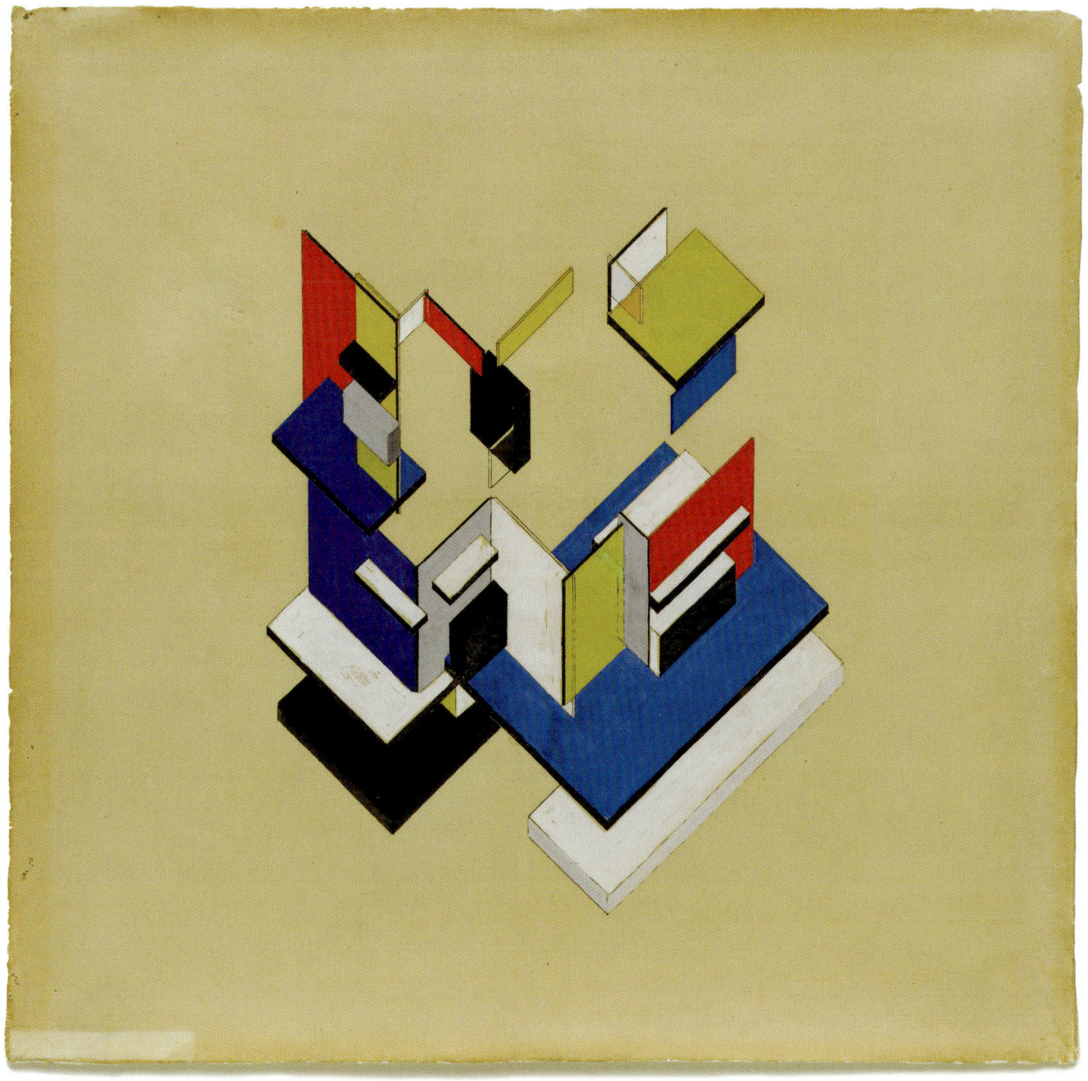

Cornelis van Eesteren and Theo van Doesburg: Contra-Construction Project, Axonometric, 1923, by permission of Museum of Modern Art, Architecture and Design Dept., New York

Quincho Jorge Newberry, Rafeal Iglesia
Rosario, 2001

Quincho Sol de Mayo, Rafeal Iglesia
Rosario, 2002

the smaller "bedroom" can be reached via either the staircase or the elevator (ideal for freedom-seeking adolescent children or independently minded service personnel), while the "master bedroom" is located one full flight of stairs below the main loft-like living room.

Iglesia has indeed challenged the conventional apartment typology with this design, and it could well be argued that the inner life of the building coheres with its structural concept. In fact, a number of integrated concepts exist. First, there is the tension between the externally visible structural system and the vertical core. The concept for the core is carried over from Iglesia's various studies of cantilevering structures, as seen either in the dining table at the Quincho Jorge Newberry (2001) or at the Quincho Sol de Mayo (2002), both in Rosario. The core is conceived as a dense fabric around which and in which services and structure, staircases and ducts are situated. What Iglesia translates in a literal manner from the quinchos is the cantilevering kitchen/dining table, projecting in the same direction as if to mimic as miniaturized architecture the projecting floor slab of the loft and that of the external terrace.

There are few building tasks for which the simple constructional logic of placing one element on another, be that a brick or a spatial unit, would not suffice to generate an overall logical result. However, the straight-forward structural fact that a high-rise building behaves more like a perpendicularly cantilevering system relative to the earth's surface than a uni-directional compression system leads either to the widening of the high-rise's base or the equivalent structural consequences (deep piles or combined pile-raft). In many ways then, Iglesia's interest in cantilevers shows itself threefold in the Altamira high-rise: first in the kitchen/dining table, second in the floor slab of the loft and terrace, and third in the high-rise's behavior as a vertical cantilever.

The interplay of these three cantilever conceptions produces a sense of giddiness, most clearly experienced when one stands at the end of the loft-like space facing the street and certainly when one looks across the city from the penthouse. Attenuated projections, tenuous juxtapositions of structural elements, and small and large voids surround the occupant of the high-rise. The generous entrance sequence at ground level with its double-height void is matched by the triple-height penthouse unit with its vertically open ended roof terrace. These two fragmentary treatments of the "base" and the "attic" create a true, generous lightness for the whole building. Furthermore, and most conspicuously, by means of the setback from the eastern site boundary, the building sacrifices an enormous volume of its property to retain the right of having openings along the largest dimension of its site, openings that are quintessential to the clear expression of separate floor slabs.

The sliding windows, set back from the tectonic elements, and the generous glazing spanning all the voids, are positioned in such a way as to render the building in as raw as state as possible. Given the relatively moderate climate of Rosario, building construction is fortunate enough not to have to insulate every single external surface.

Altamira, Rafeal Iglesia
Rosario, 2001

Thus Altamira is what you see. Iglesia has composed the building's volume in such a way as to set the entire configuration back from the visible site boundary and in turn to set back each glazing plane behind the tectonic elements, thus permitting each floor level to be distinguishable.

Besides the two quinchos and Altamira, Rafael Iglesia has viewed the structural performance of tectonic elements in radically different ways in a subsequent project for the Pabellón en el Parque de Diversiones (Pavilion in the Amusement Park, 2005, Rosario). If the idea of compressing a

Banco de Londres y América del Sud, Clorindo Testa, Sanchez Elia, Peralta Ramos y Agostini
Buenos Aires, 1959–66

cantilevering table among some much smaller wooden square sections, all held down by the weight of the concrete roof, governed the first quincho (as well as an earlier project for a staircase), then the pavilion in the amusement park further explores the primal notion of

Biblioteca Nacional de la República Argentina, Clorindo Testa, Francesco Bullrich, Alicia Cazzaniga
Buenos Aires, 1961, 1971–92

statics through simple compressive weight. The concrete roof and wall structure are seen to bear on the sawed, bark-covered tree trunks. When the pavilion is seen in the context of the surrounding trees, the trunks are an obvious choice of vertical supports. Here as elsewhere, for Iglesia, the problem of structure is the solution.

Such short-circuiting of problems requires a dose of audacity. Iglesia's attitude to statics is not to overturn its logic, since the defiance of gravity would be reckless. Instead, his concept of structural systems in these projects ensures their visceral appreciation.

Undoubtedly, the long tradition of audacious architecture in Argentina has cultivated an open mind for structural interpretations. The two most astonishing works of the immediate mid-20th century are the Banco de Londres y América del Sud (1959–66, Clorindo Testa, Sanchez Elia, Peralta Ramos y Agostini) and the Biblioteca Nacional de la República Argentina (1961, 1971–92, Clorindo Testa, Francesco Bullrich, Alicia Cazzaniga), both located in Buenos Aires. As realized designs, both large buildings predate by a decade the more well-known Centre Pompidou (1971–76, Richard Rogers and Renzo Piano) or Lloyds Building (1978–86, Richard Rogers Partnership). The size and volume of the Banco de Londres allows for a division of structural labor such that there are primary circulation cores, perimeter supports, and subsidiary structural elements such as tension rods and compression posts, akin to stalactites and stalagmites, for intermediate suspended or propped galleries.

Rather than following the orthodoxy of the modernist-rationalistic constructional system of the Maison Domino, the Banco de Londres both explores the differentiation possible given the building's size and answers public expectations for a modern banking hall. While the unprecedented openness of the bank's interior is taken for granted in the 21st century by anyone entering the space, the reverse panopticon, so to speak, from the point of view of the customer, must have had a disarming effect for banking employees. The creation of spatial effects benefitting the clarification or re-establishment of social relations has been one of the achievements of the Banco de Londres.

At the National Library, the dramatic separation of an ivory tower reading room from the underground storage-cum-treasure trove through the monumental portico serves to fix the library visitor both in the nexus of the city and indeed at the aleph, as described by Borges: at the point at which the entire universe is revealed at once.

Rafael Iglesia's approach to his pavilions for Rosario's amusement park is reminiscent of the Banco de Londres' structural interplay. Iglesia's contribution to the global architectural discourse could be argued to have been initiated in his research on cantilevers, specifically for the cantilevered wooden staircase (1998, Rosario). This line of research has been fruitful, as Altamira underscores. Although Iglesia might not lay claim to the structural pathos of the Banco de Londres and the Biblioteca Nacional, there is an intention to regard the structural performance of Altamira as an instrument of consciousness through which the subject might view the world in another light. Altamira, in the most extreme interpretation, could be sensed as a series of diving boards.

For Louis Sullivan, the ideal of an architect was not one who was "accomplished or trained," but one who has a "strong, natural liking for buildings, and a disposition to shape them in what seems to his unaffected nature a direct and simple way. He will probably tread an innocent path from his problem to its solution, and therein he will show an enviable gift of logic."[3] Thus, beginning with the innermost functions—the variable loft typology that questions the nuclear family centered around a kitchen, sanitary and staircase cores, combining the structural system of the cantilever with a helical stacking of beams and walls—Rafael Iglesia has trodden a path toward an unwitting conclusiveness to the high-rise's purpose, thus establishing "a true normal type."

Altamira, in very simple, even crude terms, conforms to the abstract tripartite division that obsessed Sullivan and his colleagues in the design of high-rises. Other high-rises have had horizontal floors, even cantilevering sections, but none have stated in such clear and emphatic terms elevated living above the ground plane. And rather than styling the verticality of the high-rise building by continuous mullions as the neo-Gothic and Miesian architects did, the sense of elevation is paradoxically more strongly established by insisting on a tenuous horizontal extension with framed views.

Thus, after over one century of Sullivan's reflections on the tall building and after half a century of Miesian abstraction of the classical Doric column, Altamira demonstrates that the thinking and building of high-rises has not come to an end. Altamira stands for an unusual instance in which approach, contents, program, siting, configuration, structure, tectonics, and detailing have all come together to conspire in a building of unusual integrity. In turn, Altamira will be a guide for high-rise conception for some time to come.

3. Sullivan, "The Tall Office Building Artistically Considered," p. 405.

Essay

A Propositional Architecture

Federico Pastorino

Within the Argentinian context, where almost all building is privately financed and where economy governs architecture, a group of works by Rafael Iglesia exists outside this system. The Altamira high-rise is part of this group of works. Here, Iglesia alters the conventional residential building typology. Among the most notable aspects of this building are its structural exploration, its re-interpretation of the residential program, its use of materials, and its coherent expression of details.

According to Fernando Diez, architectural critic and editor of the Argentinian journal *Summa+*, architecture can be classified into two types: propositional architecture and production architecture.

In most cases, the repetitive and systematic economy of production that generates urban housing allows defects that prevent reflection on the possibility of new architectural proposals. This type of architecture could be classified as production architecture. The other category takes a different point of view, suggesting innovations beyond the status quo. Thus, within this category, the work of Rafael Iglesia carries a distinct weight and gravity, concerning itself with the rewriting of established programs and the coherent and obsessive development of details. Unequivocally, the Altamira buildling violates certain laws that are deeply rooted in repetitive production.

It is no coincidence that, in a lecture by Iglesia titled "When the Problem is the Solution," Iglesia begins by asking,

"Are there things that are completely invented? A hasty response would argue that many things have already found their final constitution. However, a closer look, as free as possible from preconceptions, can prove otherwise. The question is then to face a problem as if for the first time and to consider if it is possible that some things could be otherwise. For example, the airplane as a bird, the clip as the hand, the car as ultimately a quadruped (that is, the 20th-century horse). However, it is possible that there could still be questions asked of these objects, opening them to new developments. For example, it could be asked why a city car has to have four doors, when in fact, passengers should not get out on the side of the street. Why not three doors? Is there something more than the rapid submission to the original symmetry of quadrupeds?"

Typology: The Chorizo House

One traditional type of housing in Argentina, the so-called "chorizo house," could be defined as a Roman courtyard house split in half (Figure 2). Based on this chorizo type, and because of increased urban density, residences have successively risen in height and transformed the type to what is now called the condo building (Figure 3). This shift is a result of not only code restrictions and growing property speculation, but also a new sensitivity to ways of living as more specialized spaces where distinctions between public and private spaces are required. In effect, these condos are simply stacked housing units. These are much more confined than the chorizo house; the condo units are connected by vertical circulation and long, dark corridors, that provide access to each dwelling.

In those instances in which financial speculation and a simple veneer of aesthetic appreciation are key issues and the conceptualization and reconsideration of "dwelling" is a neglected concern, the common areas of design for this

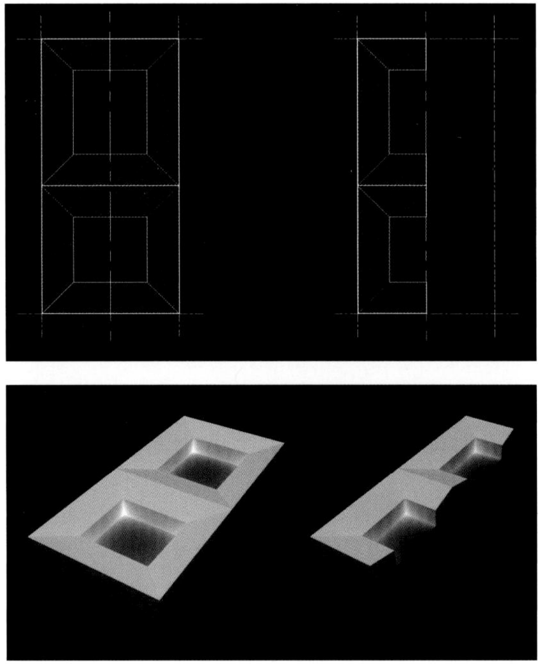

Unit Type 1 (left) and Type 2 (right)
Altamira, Rafael Iglesia, Rosario, 2001

type of production architecture are reduced to the facades, balconies and railings, and coating materials, all the while adhering to standards determined by the housing market.

In the case of the Altamira building, Iglesia reinterprets the entry and views. Furthermore, he externalizes the corridors, which in other buildings is interior; this is simply the re-instatement of the chorizo house's well-known patio, in which this exterior space gives access to each room. In the context of this reinterpretation, the chorizo house takes on a new meaning. In the past, the occupant had to traverse the patio to access the toilet or the kitchen; in the Altamira building, the occupant passes through the patio-balcony to access the dwelling unit. Furthermore, the patio-balcony allows the dwelling to expand to an outside terrace overlooking the Paraná River. This provides independence to one of the bedrooms and gives an answer to the question of the contemporary patchwork family. The patio-balcony can also accommodate a separated work space within the house. Therefore, in an unconventional way, the reworking of the chorizo house's patio resolves the problem of the dark and hidden passages of production architecture. Besides forming a non-conventional prototype in which a bedroom is detached from the hall's core, the new unit recovers the traditional four-by-four meter room dimension (as opposed to three-by-three meters in most condo developments) that in an atypical way refers to the conventional, and now highly coveted, chorizo houses.

The organization of these internally disconnected bedroom studios is resolved by stacking and joining two different housing units: Type 1, consisting of three rooms, one of which is the bedroom studio space, and Type 2, which has only one room. These units are linked by scissor stairs serving as a non-mechanical, alternative connection throughout the building and providing the Type 1 units with access to one of the bedrooms.

Structure: A Play with Forces

The structural system is comprised of a single element: the beam. The solid-void relationships are defined by the arrangement of beams; they become spatial-compositional elements. The beams are left exposed to reveal the bare structural system, clearly denoting the function of the elements that compose it. Thus, the structural arrangement defines the enclosure, provides for views out, and allows natural light to enter the space. As an explanation, Iglesia quotes Sol Lewitt:

"In a logical object each part depends on the previous one.
A certain sequence is established, based on logic.
Notwithstanding, a rational object requires that a logical decision be
Taken at each moment...

It is something which must be reflected on.
In a logical sequence reflection does not exist.
It is a way of not thinking. It is irrational."

The resolution between building and ground is one of nuance and requires one to reflect on and organize the understood logic of the building's structure. In the text entitled "HOMO-NO" (a reference to Le Corbusier's concept of the Maison DOMINO), Iglesia clarifies:

"For now, my intention is to re-think the relationship with the ground by reversing the question: I propose that weight is not the problem; rather it is the solution. I try to hold things differently, without forcing them to disclose the working muscles, and I show how the structural elements work. Instead I am interested in following the pattern of oriental fighting in which each contestant takes advantage of the strength of his opponent. These are now my reasons, in this age in which lightness is invading us."

The beams are organized in a notable way: they are stacked in the traditional manner in which logs are dried in a lumber yard. This way of stacking becomes the structural system. After a few seconds of contemplating the building, what appears confusing soon reveals a logic that amazes the eye. The observer discovers that the structural elements, the beams, are simply organized wisely.

Detail: Representing the Work Itself

The consistency of the details, understood here as the subordination of each element to represent the general logic of the work, can be clearly observed in the Altamira building.

First, the use of white paint homogenizes and unifies the work. Both the interior and exterior are the same painted white concrete, thus preserving the formal unity of the building. Second, the meeting of two chamfered pieces of glass (cut at 45°) at the southeastern corner is an exquisite detail that dematerializes the joint in a fine line; this detail accentuates the tension that the beams generate in the most exposed corner of the building. Third, on the interior, along the sides of the living room, wood floor-boards are mounted and line the wall, thereby differentiating the beam system from cladding elements. Iglesia has referred to this detail as a victory over the problem of skirting (the skirting is in this case the same floor folded vertically). In a separate building, the Independence Park Pavilion,

Unit Type 1 (top) and Type 2 (bottom)
Altamira, Rafael Iglesia, Rosario, 2001

Iglesia resolved the problem of creating lateral stability—which arises here when the concrete walls do not reach the floor, but appear floating and hang from the roof slab—by necessarily distributing the load to stabilize the tree trunks acting in compression.

At Altamira, along the living room, the metal window frames run behind the beam, leaving a narrow gap between the two elements. These two elements are thereby rendered as autonomous constructional and tectonic components. This obsession not to connect different elements to the structure is repeated in many of the window details. Most of these windows are only supported by a metal grid, for example, the pane of glass that forms a windscreen outside the elevator, the pane of glass that protects the ground floor entrance hall, or the handrails that cross the beams without touching them.

The cantilevering wooden kitchen counter, similar to the wooden floor, also seems to be a conceptual model for the entire building. The structural configuration of this puzzle subordinates the organization of all constructive elements to this conceptual model, thereby ensuring a coherent resolution.

Other Works: Same Author, Same Forces

Iglesia seems to be obsessed by such design variables as weight, gravity, beams and balances, the way in which buildings relate to the ground, and the way spaces are determined by a building's structural organization.

The cantilevering detail is also found in other projects by Iglesia: for example, the wooden stairs and the wooden tables at the two quinchos (barbecue pit pavilions, 2001 and 2002) and the large wooden table supported by stacked beams at the Independence Park Pavilion (2004). In these projects, the materials, the use of wood and concrete's natural characteristics, are taken to their limits. By knowing the physical characteristics of materials, the architect is able to combine building components to work to their utmost potential, creating a system that resolves itself structurally.

Iglesia has also created pieces of sculpture where the addition of weight resolves the structural problems. It always seems that instead of working with known solutions, he investigates well-known problems to make them resolve themselves. This play with forces is expressed in four pieces of wood that are combined in an ingenious way: the weight of one supports another, and within this closed system, the problem resolves itself.

Idependence Park Pavillion, Rafael Iglesia
Rosario, 2003

Architectural Context: Jorge Scrimaglio and Marcelo Villafañe

Iglesia is not in favor of being classified or merged with three other architects—Solano Benitez of Paraguay, Angelo Bucci of Brazil, and Alejandro Aravena of Chile—as he often is. In the text "America no del Norte," a response to the essay "Latin American Scream and Silence," he states, "First, I think it's a superstition, an excessive search for an alleged identity that only holds in relation to space and the human need to classify." In this article, Iglesia clarifies his position with this assessment:

"It is like thinking that those who live in a city have certain characteristics or, more specifically, those who inhabit the city center are different from those who live in neighborhoods; children living in the same street are more similar to each other than with respect to those who live around the corner, and those living in the same building are the same. And I do not tell you about those who live on the same floor: they are all identical. Thus, one ends up sleeping with oneself, that is to say alone. If all men are equal, a view I share with Marx and the feminists, this seems an exaggeration."

Trying to find a common space with other Latin American architects, Iglesia prefers to speak of affinities, concerns, and needs. Although he considers these associations important, they must all understand architecture as a social tool and not merely as a formal appearance.
In comparing Iglesia to other colleagues who have a common conceptual belief about architecture and construction, another possible "group" can be found. This group of colleagues is characterized by its use of resourceful research into construction materials (wood, concrete, brick,

House of Norberto Alorda, Jorge Scrimaglio
Rosario, 1968-1973

etc). Jorge Scrimaglio and Marcelo Villafañe, along with others, are surely part of this group of architectural investigators, who also share the city in which they live: Rosario. In the case of Scrimaglio, the brick is the main protagonist; in the case of Villafañe, it is laminated wood. In all cases, these investigations use material by exposing their limits of applicability within the architectural space. Iglesia explains further:

"A window is always a window, a door is a door, a roof, a roof. Each is a subject of the statement provided with a relative meaning, and those meanings are agreed on a designated subject. In Scrimaglio's architecture, by contrast, what is at stake is not these elements, but bricks, simple arithmetic units whose function is anonymous, collective, third person. A brick is turned into a subjective element that has no intrinsic properties except one that is given as a result of its situation: "it" can be floor, ceiling, stair, window, wall eventually, according to its place in space. In this scarcity of resources, the work finds its richness and its unity in diversity, since it is one and one all at once."

"It"—the insistent brick—breaks, covers, borders, rises, falls, maintains, retains, supports, is absent, is gone, without altering the unit. But the minimum real unit is not the brick itself, but rather its behavior within the tissue—in the text, which is a single point intertwined with the other, where the detail is indistinguishable from the whole; that is to say, we could build on the exception, build the system. The "brick" is one of those characters that can be the hero or the steward who appears and disappears in the plot, as necessary for the fulfillment of destiny.

In the case of the Altamira building, Iglesia plays with the elements in the same way, disarming their systems of meaning, or at least becoming more complex and ambiguous: the beams are also the building envelope or the floor is the baseboard and vertical closure at the same time. In the text, "Latin American Architecture (Whales, Butterflies, Camels, Among Other Things)," Iglesia reflects:

"We are more geographical than historical (we do not have a past that connects us). The landscape is what makes us countrymen. And this somehow implies common viewpoints. And the fact of seeing the same window makes us assume that we are a people under one roof."

Perhaps this is the reason for linking these three architects; the same landscape, Rosario, distinguishes them from the rest. It is a landscape that has always had a rich and purposeful cultural production, including music, visual arts, and literature. This group of architects that lives in Rosario, while designing different architecture and producing different research, finds common ground in the creation of architecture as research.

Proposal: A Reflection of Our Times

Iglesia's way of creating architecture, where reflection and research find its fullest expression with a rhythm that does not denote urgency, differentiates his work from production architecture.

The lock, the counterweight, material investigation, wit, and the unknown are just some ideas that may describe Iglesia's work; they also qualify his work as research and propositional architecture. For this reason Fernando Diez says in "Architecture and Danger," that this way of making architecture leads Iglesia to produce the most successful and most eloquent piece of concrete since the Banco de Londres y America del Sud (1959–66) by SEPRA/Clorindo Testa. Again, in the text "HOMO-NO" Iglesia says,

"This is what Le Corbusier did in life. But much time has passed since those days; however, we continue to produce along the same principles of construction on which a society that no longer exists was once founded. I think it is time to reinterpret the past and to break with tradition, just as our hero did in his time."

What Iglesia is proposing in his text and in his buildings is the same: when faced with construction, instead of producing naïve replicas without reflection, the architect has an opportunity to ask questions. Iglesia is looking for logical ways to reflect our times, wisely researching the use of a material, taking into account the physical, chemical, and even social aspects:

"This runs through my own work, that it has always been the case in architecture to support a roof, which is to say, to carry a weight (the toiling Caryatids prove what I say). From the outset it has always been a struggle of forces in which only one outcome is possible: to win (otherwise, the ceiling collapses). Architecture's raison d'etre is to provide a roof for a diverse and classified world."

From the way this weight is held, a thousand and one theories have been made, spanning from the era of the dolmens to today. According to the technology available to humans in each era, changes in the relationship to the ground plane have changed—the pulley and lever decomposed and created new possibilities. For example, for the inclined plane, specific machines were invented to enable the Pyramids to be built; the Roman arch expanded the opening; the dome and the wide roof generated spaces without columns; the Gothic arch, the parabola of Gaudí gained height, and ultimately iron and concrete allowed architecture to scrape the sky, but always with its feet on the ground.

Once at Buenos Aires University, Iglesia commented that, for him, there are two ways of making architecture: one disciplinary and another professional. His work focuses on the disciplinary way of the researcher without simply submitting to market laws. In his search, propositions are made and risks are taken, but when these risks are overcome and they transcend conventions, they become part of a new universal architecture.

Altamira

Rafael Iglesia

In a logical object each part depends on the previous one.
A certain sequence is established, based on logic.
Notwithstanding, a rational object requires that a logical decision be
Taken at each moment…
It is something which must be reflected on.
In a logical sequence reflection does not exist.
It is a way of not thinking. It is irrational.

— Sol Lewitt

In this project I intended to highlight two aspects above the others: First, I questioned what defines an apartment and how it works. Second, I investigated unique structural solutions.

The Program

The Modern Movement left us not only its aesthetics, but also its ethics. Thus, in a dwelling, functionalism and the specificity of function required a room for parents (for procreation) and another for children (two rooms, if they were of different sexes). With the Altamira building, I question this functional specificity (and its ethical implications). The traditional family unit is no longer what it used to be, and this change may be traced to ethics. Unfortunately, we cannot argue ethics here.

Structure

In his seminal writings, the late 20th-century French philosopher Gilles Deleuze wrote a description of two games of opposing function. These two games, chess and go, can be used to illustrate two ways of working within architecture. In chess, the pieces have innate properties that govern how they behave. In go, the positions of the pieces have more influence on behavior.

In a codified architecture, all its elements operate as the chess pieces: they have an inner nature, or intrinsic properties, that define what they are. Thus a window is always a window, a door is a door, a beam is a beam, and this is true with every component in a building. These components have designed roles, movements, and positions. Each of them is subject to their particular definition, with all their particular meanings combined into the role of defining what "building" is.

With the Altamira building, I aimed to achieve the opposite. Much as Deleuze describes the game go, I am trying to show only that the beams, treated as simple units in which function is undefined, can be treated as collective and adaptable. Here, beams are not defined as subjects with intrinsic properties. Their properties derive from their situation: beams may become a wall, a window, or a door. Perhaps, they will act their roles—for example, to support something—but those roles will depend on the specific space they occupy. Thus the persistent beam moves around, constructing, destroying, skirting, going up and down, supporting, lingering, and disappearing when least expected—all without altering the unity of the building. Within the work, the beam may become the hero or the butler, appearing or disappearing only to fulfill the requirement of destiny.

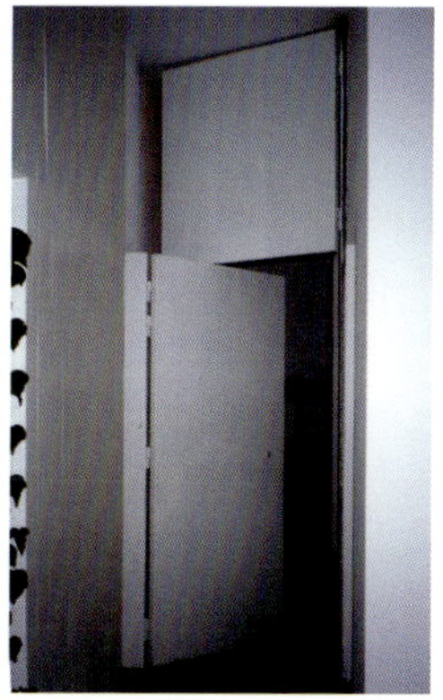

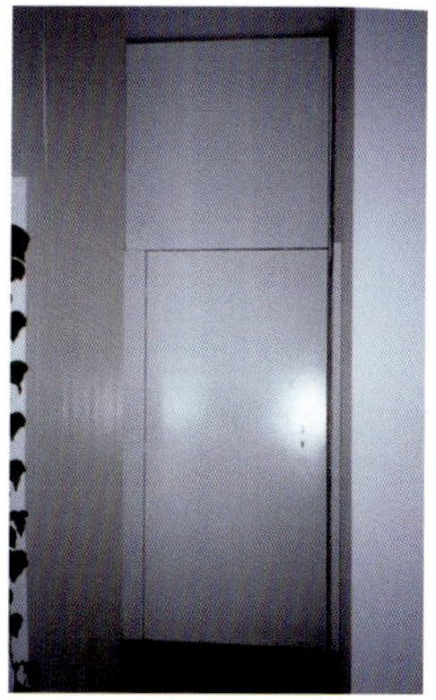

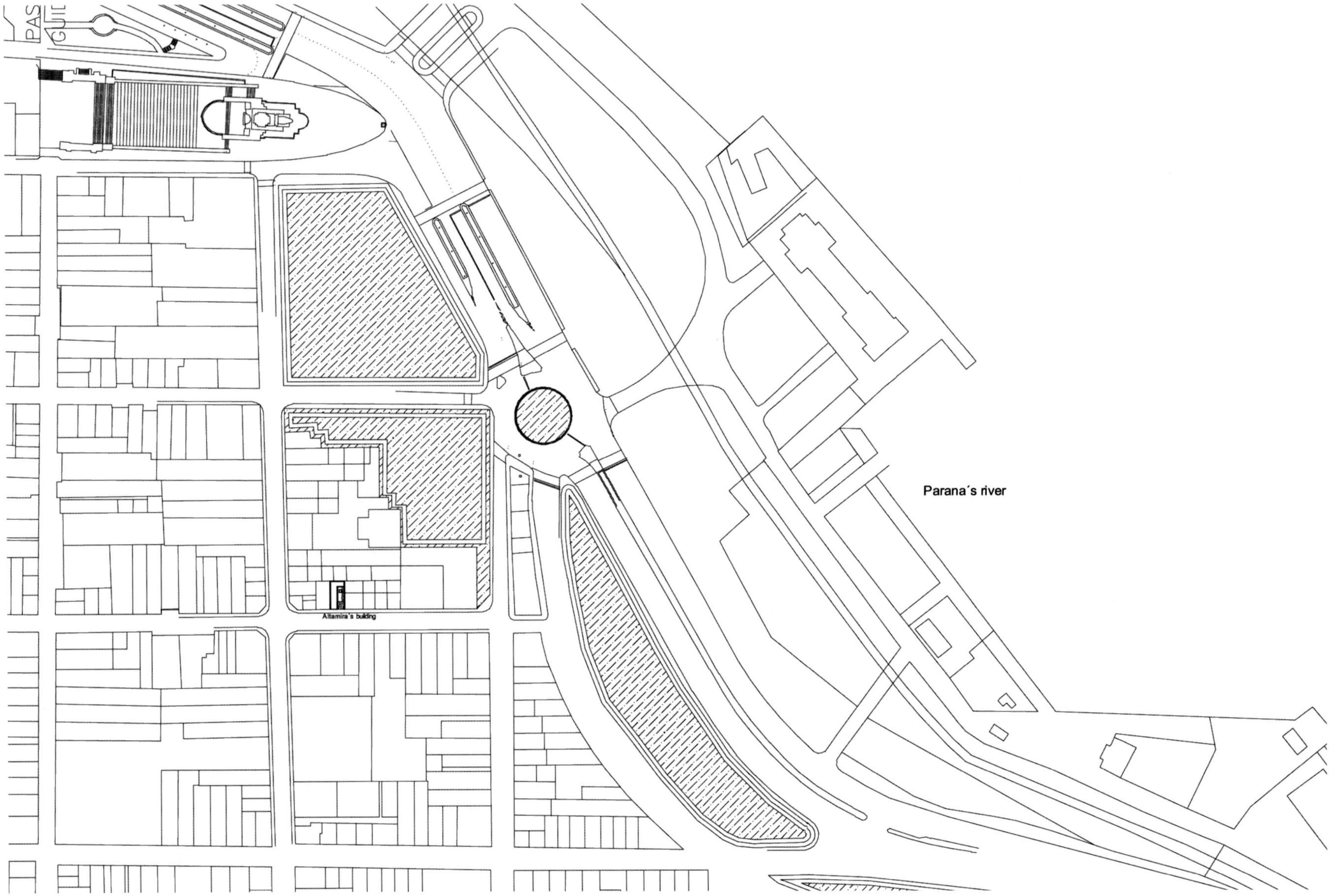
Parana´s river
Altamira´s building

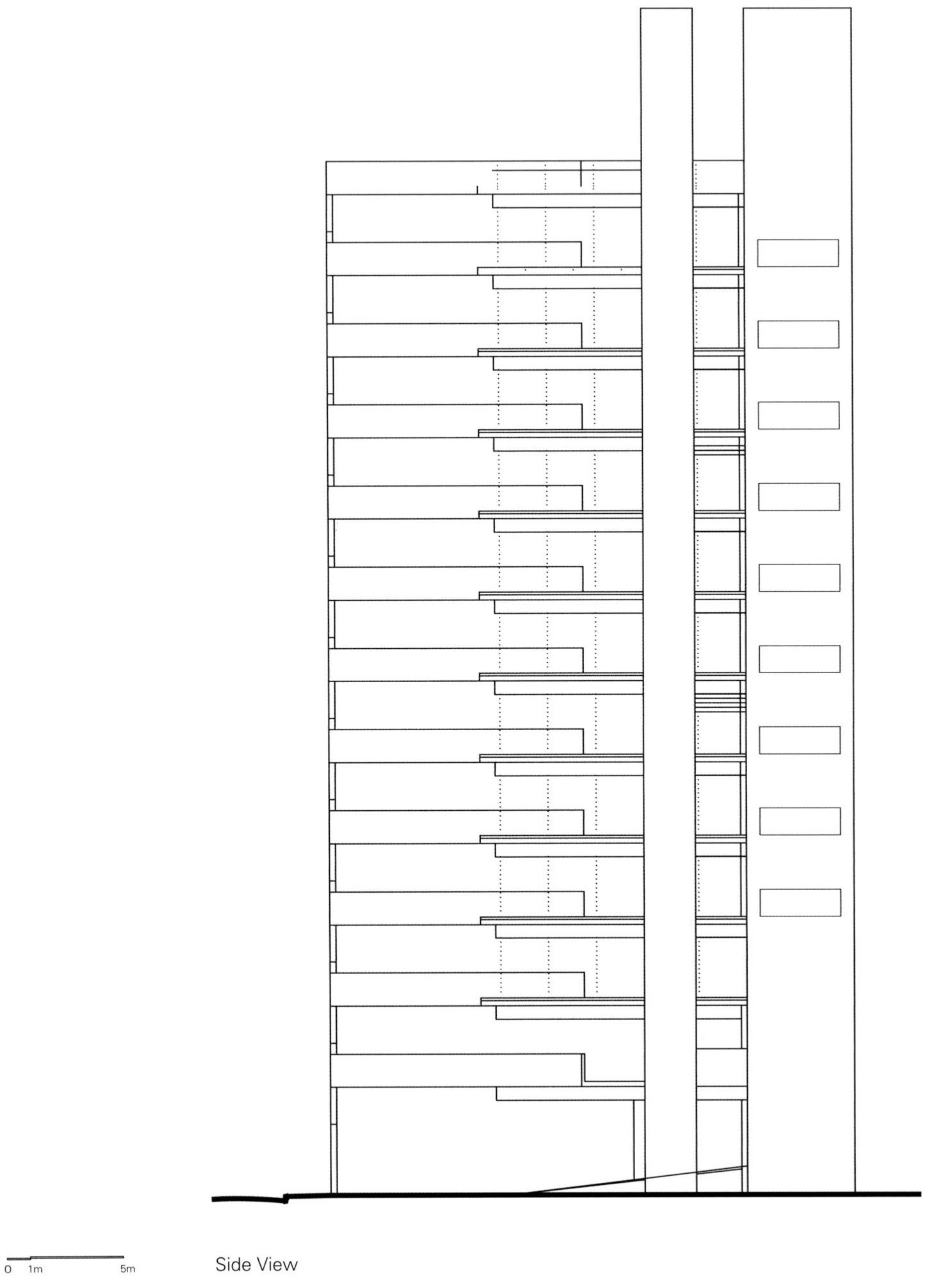

Side View

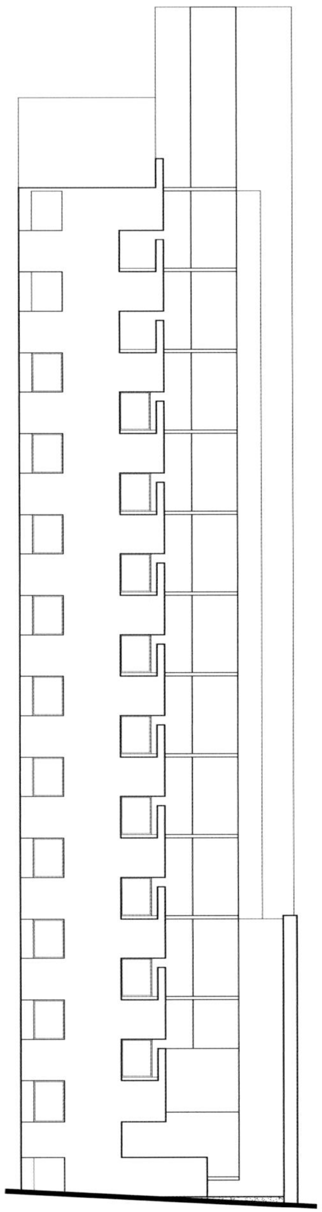

Front View

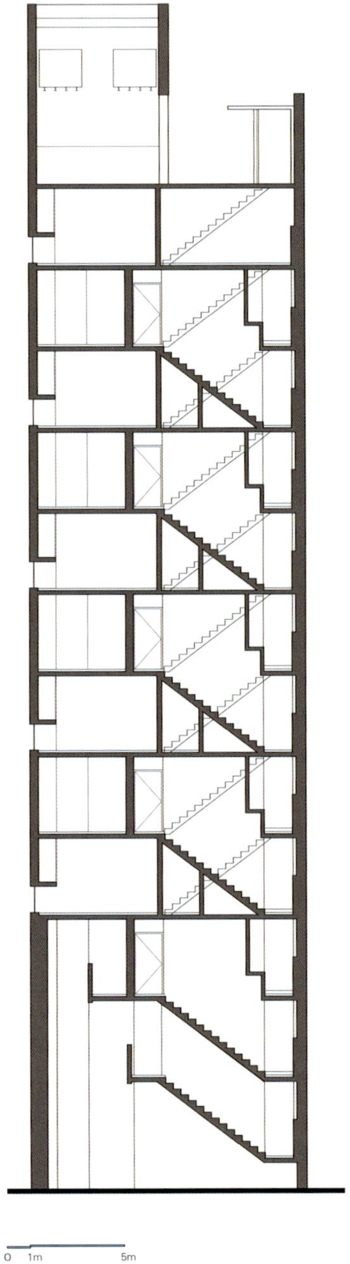

Section AA

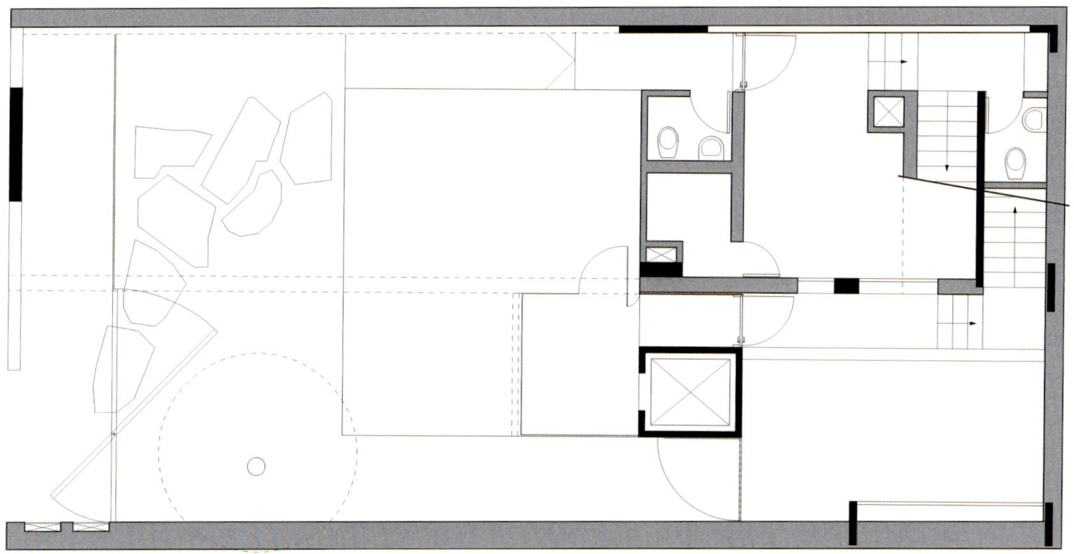

Floor Plan – Entrance

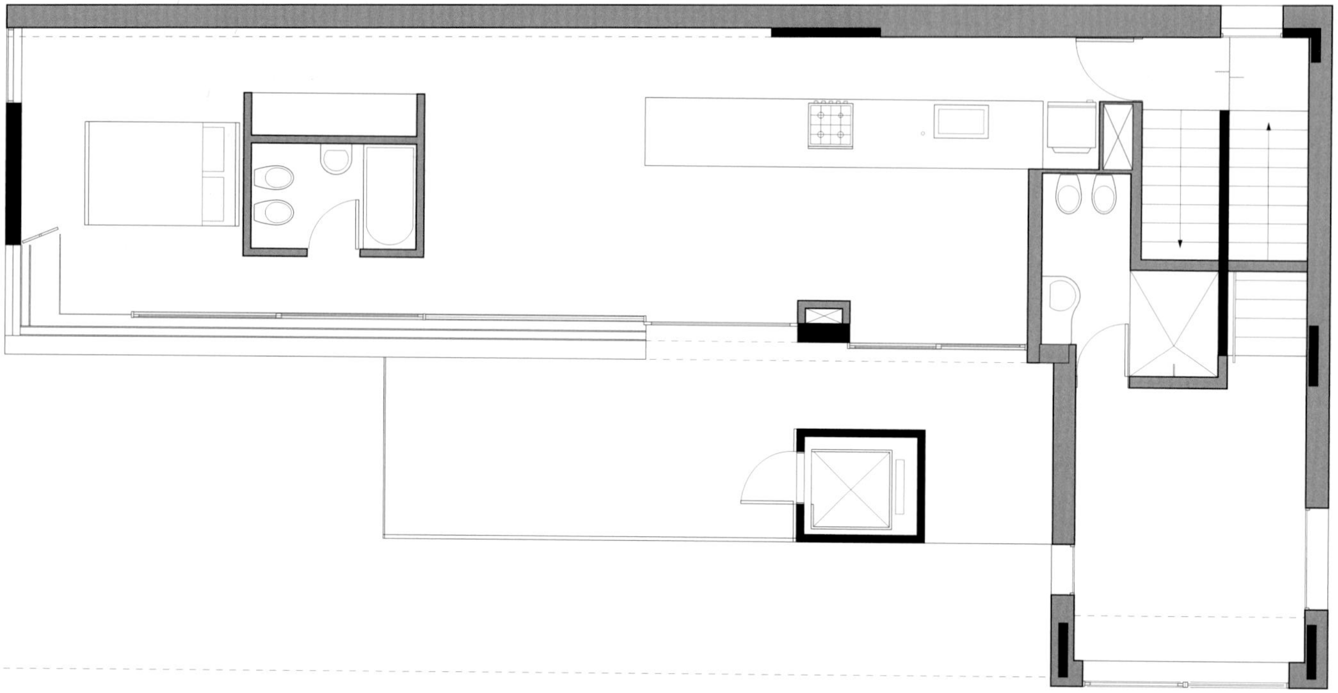

Floor Plan – Levels 3, 5, 7 and 9

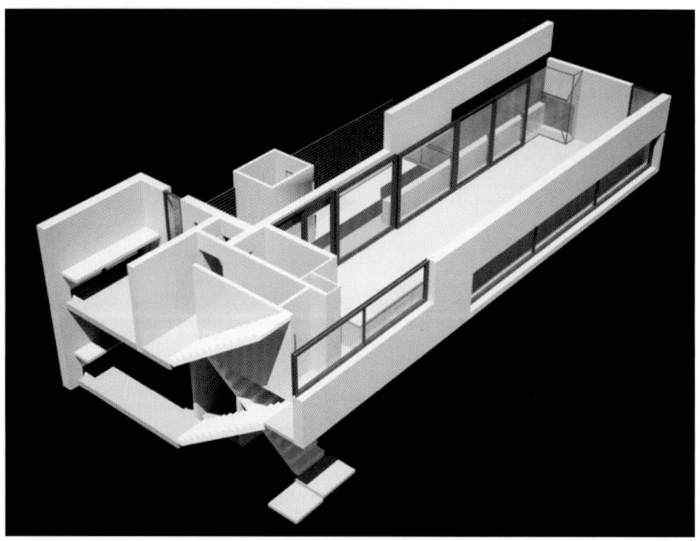

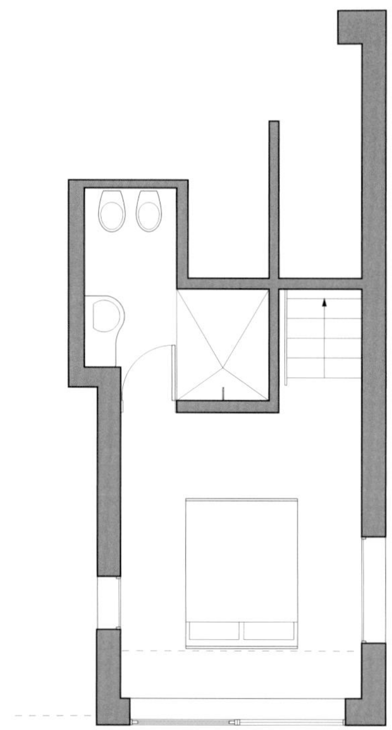

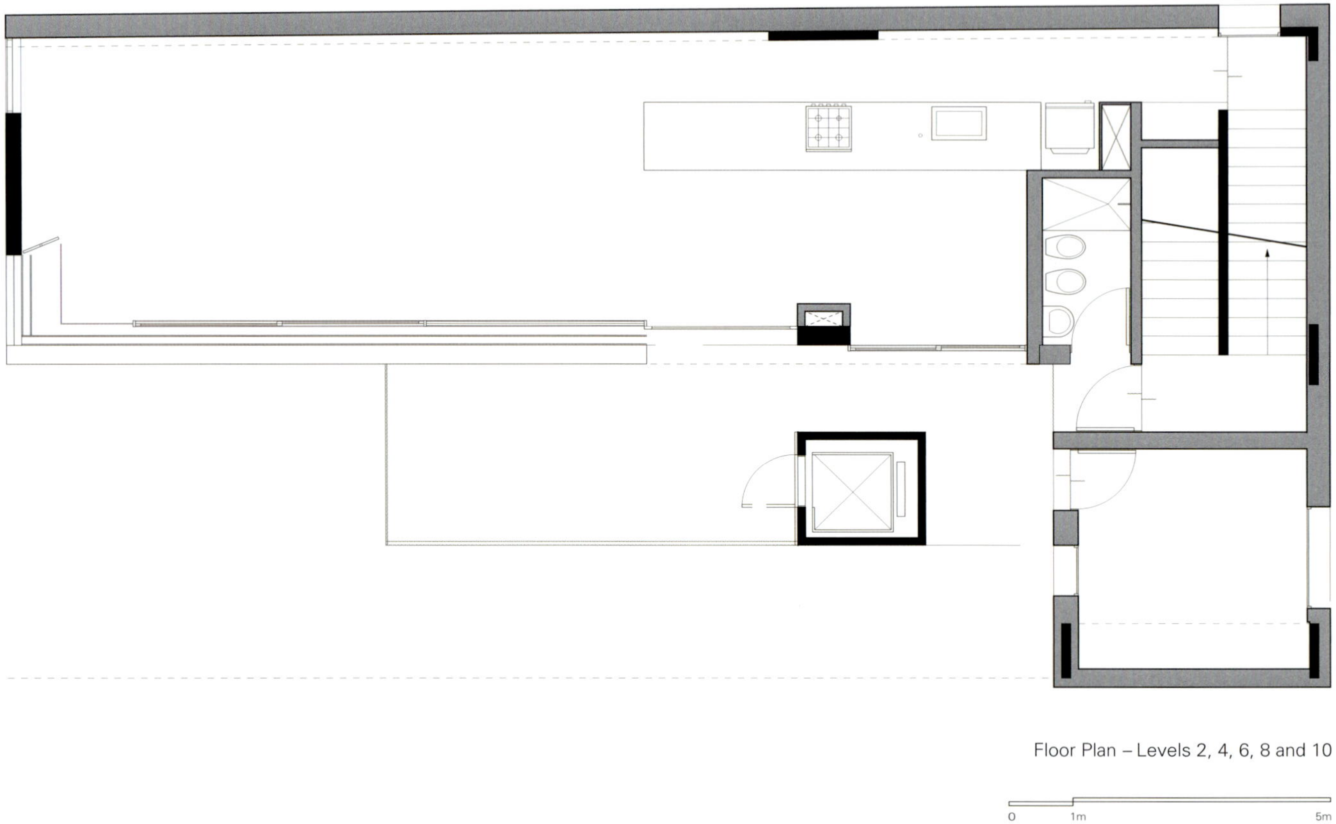

Floor Plan – Levels 2, 4, 6, 8 and 10

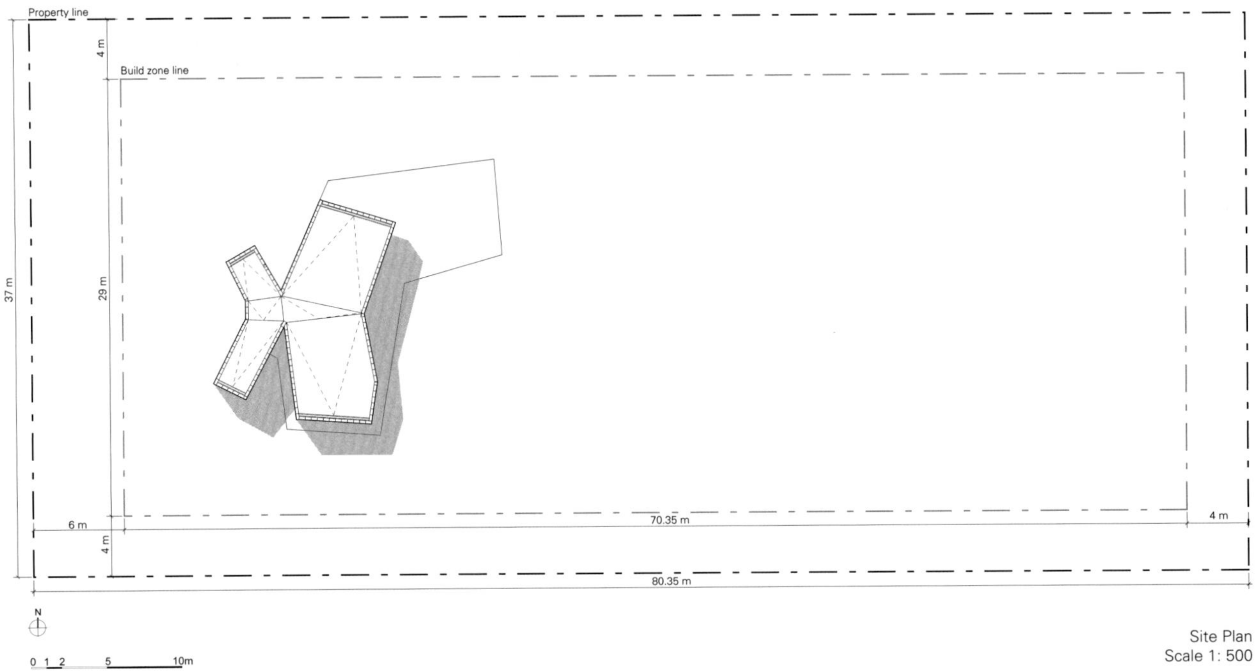

Site Plan
Scale 1: 500

Florencia Raigal House in Rosario, 2005 – 2006
Marcelo Villafañe

Marcelo Villafañe in his studio
Rosario, 2007

Essay

Roofs That Know How To Fly

Juan Manuel Rois

Among other activities, Marcelo Villafañe paints and plays soccer.

As with some extraordinary people, with Villafañe it is difficult to separate the architect from the architecture. Consequently, it is necessary to introduce biographic information in order to contextualize the design of the roofs of his recent houses, those roofs seemingly twisted by the Pampas winds.

Beginnings

Before becoming an architect, Marcelo Villafañe was a national, award-winning painter.

At the end of the 1960s, his vocation in this plastic art was inspired by the unorthodox teaching methods of the Rosarinean painter Julio Vanzo. At his master's library, the young Villafañe would spend hours browsing through books, absorbing. Afterwards, back in his own studio, he would paint. His first paintings demonstrated an abstract expressionism combined with an underlying figuration depicting some of the marginal inhabitants of the working-class outskirts of Rosario.

Another figure weighs heavily on Villafañe's formation: Lucio Fontana. He was a constant presence at Vanzo's studio; Fontana's bust of Vanzo's head was the testimony of the friendship without borders between these two great men. The vital force of Fontana, the Argentinean-Italian master, and his intuitive, primordial work are foundational marks on Villafañe.

Marcelo Villafañe was a student at the School of Architecture in Rosario in the early 1970s, a tumultuous period. It was a time of revolutionary claims: for art without brushes, for architecture to dissolve into sociology, for schools as collectives without hierarchical boundaries between student and teacher. In the middle of this political storm, Augusto Pantarotto emerged as a figure of architectural disciplinary resistance, a modern architect with modern ideas. He was a professor for the last year of Villafañe's academic career and remained a strong point of reference for him.

Parallel to this political movement, Villafañe had a breakthrough. He discovered the work of a strange local figure, architect Jorge Scrimaglio, and soon chose Scrimaglio as his architectural guide. At a distance, but meticulously, he would study every building under construction designed by this elusive character. This pursuit has been an ever revelatory but unending mystery, even after 30 years. This quest has delivered intellectual suspense of low tension without resolution.

Villafañe's respect for vernacular construction techniques comes as a consequence of his interest in Scrimaglio. In the almost primitive buildings of Scrimaglio, vernacular techniques are imbedded in contemporary architectural propositions by way of an uncompromising quest for abstraction.

Finally, in the middle of the 1970s, Villafañe found refuge in the systemic temporary structures of Julio Bruguera. From his buildings in Buenos Aires comes Villafañe's understanding of the creative and spatial freedoms afforded by playful variations under the premises of rigorous geometric and tectonic systems. This is another of the foundational moments currently finding a final synthesis in Villafañe's most recent work.

Phases

Villafañe develops his work in series.

In a series, architectural problems are translated from work to work. The collection of these works gives perspective and offers the possibility of enunciating particulars and refinements that produce variations within the group. Sometimes the themes lose their intensity, and the series comes to an end.

In his architectural practice, after an initial period based on the material differentiations of clearly articulated volumes in counter-intuitive combinations, Marcelo Villafañe entered a transitional phase, his period of white houses.

Casa Seoane (1) of 1991 represents the highest point of this exploration of elemental geometric rigor and explicit urban commitment. In this house, the dense orthogonal urban grain of the center of a Rosarinean city block is sublimated by extending the height of some of the walls beyond what is reasonable or necessary. These are fake party walls that play against the blue sky in a game of perspective with those real and far away. With its multiplication of the party wall to the point of absurdity, this house invites the others into a freer, more conceptual game.

Casa Seoane, Marcelo Villafañe
Rosario, 1991

In this period of restricted architecture, Villafañe continued to paint and exhibit his work. While Villafañe-as-painter explored expansive and expressionist geometries, Villafañe-as-architect rigorously controlled his urban pieces, disciplined and built inside the framework of the urban reality of Rosario.

Systematic Chaos

Villafañe needs organization.

He creates methods to seemingly organize in order to playfully experiment. These systems of organization are proportional systems, geometric games of relationships, and plastic formal structures.

In a very opportunistic way, for these last ten years, Villafañe has pursued a parallel project; utilizing moments of otherwise unimportant commissions, he has developed variations on a material exploration with plywood sheets. His is a tectonic system based upon modular repetition and the accumulation and separation of material. Here the literal operation of rotation is also a conceptual inversion: the internal layers of the plywood sheet are exposed, almost exponentially multiplying the cut texture of the material. Natural light, filtering through the interstitial spaces, activates the multiplicity of internal lines and finished surfaces. This tectonic system has been used to materialize decks, screens, doors, tables, and most importantly, staircases. Multiple variations of these staircases exist: solid or ethereal ones, hanging or freestanding ones, with apparent or hidden metallic supports, dark or clear ones. In these staircases, the material rotates in friction, creating visual games of apparent instability.

Villafañe establishes material systems that work by pure construction; they are architectural machines that establish a territory for exploration. The proliferation of the module constructs a pattern, an abstract spatial system that is clearly tectonic. His playful drive for exploration extends the operation beyond its logical limits: by using procedural abstraction, he arrives at pure expressive machines. Villafañe smiles, while he plays seriously.

Paradoxically, this systemic tectonic experimentation opened the doors for the design of a more recent series of houses of formless plants and fluid roofs.

Displacements

The last series of paintings by Villafañe (long interrupted but recently reinitiated) are big canvases of dark background where, defined by trembling and shining lines, strange horizontal figures float. These are organs without body, perspectives without architecture. It is this painterly, formal impulse that erupts in Villafañe's architecture, finally obliterating all separations between seemingly disparate modes of artistic practice.

A geographic factor of displacement also functions as a trigger for this final transformation.

Villafañe is an architect of houses, and recently his clientele has preferred the gated communities on the outskirts of the city. For Rosario, the outskirts mean the big open plains of the Pampas. Soon his architecture will no longer be the wise and rigorous game of urban volumes under the Rosarinean vertical light, but rather extended bodies on the flat Pampas receiving the low setting sun.

Florencia Raigal House, plywood stair detail, Marcelo Villafañe
Rosario, 2006

Casa Seoane (2), Marcelo Villafañe
Rosario, 2000

Casa Seoane (2), finished in 2000 inside the gated community of the Kentucky Country Club, exposes the logic determining the field of experimentation for a new series of buildings: a contemporary reinterpretation of the popular typology of the Pampas ranch. In this series, the houses are objects against the horizon, and they delineate place by the creation of shade. These houses are defined, low-edged roofs with high ridges conforming to pleated geometries of slightly pitched planes. These metal roofs are independent of the rest of the structure: steel tube columns support a frame of metallic tubes with big sections spanning long distances in contrast to the small scale of the houses. Here, the innovative structural separation between roof and perimeter walls allows the CMU walls to move freely in search of views, orientation, and privacy.

In Casa Seoane (2), at the highest point of the roof ridge, the CMU wall functions as support; it is only here that wall and structure coincide. This is a brief moment, for suddenly we see how the wall separates in plan and section from the roof: a bifurcation that creates spatial continuity and a multiplication of diagonal lines in the generous interior space. The burnished plywood beams, the black metallic tubes, and the white CMU walls all continue along their way in apparent freedom. Every piece follows its own material and geometric game. We understand that they are playing in concert with one another, but it is difficult for us to decipher where they are going. The plywood ceiling, escaping from the living room towards the veranda, guides our view towards the line of eucalyptus trees in front of the sunset horizon.

With the same cheap materials and vernacular construction techniques, Casa Brown (2002) is a Pampas ranch that grew into a manor house. Here, we find an innovation that is fundamental for the further development in the series: the ridge will no longer necessarily be horizontal. In this way, the houses are no longer normalized objects. With this simple gesture of deformation, they acquire a biological character: the ridge is now the spinal column of a giant armadillo. They become prehistoric animals moving in geological time across the Pampas.

Casa Brown is big enough to curl into itself. In spiral continuity from the highest ridge point, the lowest roof edge protects a porch and folds towards the pivoting moment of the L-shaped plan. With this movement, and some precise cuts and fissures, a typical corner L-shaped plan gains spatial complexity, while protecting small introverted courtyards and bringing native vegetation to the kitchen. In the apparently free-flowing CMU walls, profound horizontal views in diagonal create a choreography of apertures that let us see the treetops against the blue sky or the horizon beyond the low veranda. A horizontal axis of symmetry organizes a dark wood ceiling and its dark wood floor counterpart, both separated by white painted walls inundated by light. All this is achieved with a precise control of spatial relationships that create a contemporary, domestic, interior space full of serenity and Argentinean Creole elegance.

Casa Brown, Marcelo Villafañe
Rosario, 2002

The Florencia Raigal House demonstrates a high degree of concentration, unusual for a house so small. This house is a synthesis of ideas—an architectural manifesto.

A maximum variation within the series, the Florencia Raigal House replaces the light corrugated metal roof of previous houses with a concrete slab contained within CMU walls by a low parapet. With its walls and roof of the same material and monochromatically coded, the house presents itself from the distance as a monolith, as a stone fallen from the sky, a meteorite. How do we explain our surprise when entering the house? Once inside, we do not quite understand how a house that small could, in fact, protect a huge interior space. What game of proportions is the architect playing to be able to produce such a compact space, at the same time so monumental and so cozy?

In this house with a double-bifurcated plan; the two small wings protect the big western-facing windows in the main interior space. These windows, enormous in relation to the space they are in, are in perfect caliber with the interior circulation defined by the plywood staircase. Coming or going, we look through the windows at deep oblique angles. Our gaze, protected and framed by the house itself, escapes toward the far away horizon.

The plan bifurcation repeats the angles of the pitched roof; the same geometry defines the horizontal and the vertical plane. This object under the sun receives its own shadow. During the course of the day, new diagonal lines complete the geometry and multiply the variety of views. When walking in circles around it, one never sees this friendly house the same way. It does not matter how many times we visit, this house will always surprise us with a new face.

Casa Begué (2007) is the last work in the series. A light variation showcasing the ease of a master at play, the house scatters its green walls in precise ways. Villafañe bifurcates its roofs and unfolds its plan to let us in on a narrow moment: the pivot of the main door places us in front of a big window looking out again. After repositioning our bodies, we notice we are already under the highest point of the ceiling ridge in a unified interior space of unexpected dimensions and warmth. From this space, our gaze moves a full 360 degrees, always finding a window to escape toward the surrounding horizon.

To Play Seriously/in Series

Following the logic of the formal/material system with playful ease, Marcelo Villafañe arrives at conceptual leaps. He works under self-imposed rules like a jazz musician plays a standard: he knows how to begin, and he knows where to end, but in between is a journey full of improvisation and variation. This search propels him into uncharted territories.

Villafañe plays. He plays the way Enric Miralles invited all of us to play: seriously. Like the best Argentinean soccer players that he so fully admires, Villafañe plays with technical precision and elegance, with clear strategies and freedom of action. We see in this way of practicing architecture a spatial and tectonic imagination, one both conceptual and material. This is architectural thinking in action with disciplinary rigor and maximum creative freedom.

Villafañe has written about his intention to work between a systematic order and a broken grid. The production of chaotic variations within logical systems brings Villafañe to new, less formal orders. It is here that Villafañe finds himself at ease.

Essay

Florencia Raigal House

WIlfried Wang

If we take a moment to reflect on the design and construction of houses—a building type that has been the canvas upon which so many clients and architects have tested their visions—for each of us, images and experiences of quotidian and ambitious examples cross our minds. From palatial-wannabe to rural retreat, from haute-bourgeois self-proclamation to transcendental weekend lodge, we may recall all hues of lifestyle possibilities.

Occasionally, the house is more a quiet background, a recessive stage, upon which a specific lifestyle is enacted. At other times, it is the main feature; it is the protagonist of the client and architect's dramatic enactment of their vision of life and the inhabitants are mere extras providing a semblance of purpose.

Andrea Palladio's villas mapped an idea of anti-urban Christian order onto the Venetian hinterland so as to rise to a form of redemption by cultivating people and territory. Frank Lloyd Wright's Usonian houses and his vision for Broadacre City offered a similarly self-sufficient ideal, but now following the concept of a real-estate determined democratization of Jeffersonian persuasion, a more widely shared suburban life, a vision that, during Wright's time, was already becoming a reality in the Anglo-Saxon world. Adolf Loos' few houses were exceptions in the way that they were spatially compacted inventions of quasi late Austro-Hungarian courtly manners—mute or even autistic to the outside. Loos' contained houses could exist both in urban and suburban contexts. A similar condition exists in Ludwig Mies van der Rohe's houses: distinct from the apartments within the high-rises, which sought the earth's horizon, all of his later houses were conceived within smaller or larger enclosed boundaries (including the Farnsworth House, a fully glazed building set inside a large private property). A review of the entire spectrum of realized house constuction shows that, a century after classical modernism, the haute-bourgeois lifestyle embedded in the houses of the classical modernists, while persisting in some larger mansions being constructed, is receding.

At the same time, the recession of the haute-bourgeois aspect does not seem to diminish the desire among some clients to adhere to this mentality's representative desire. The result of this disparity—shrinkage and simplification of spatial program while insisting on communicating ideas of wealth and sophistication—is the core architectural struggle: how does the architect deal with the allure of grandeur in vestigial forms? For architects aware of these opposing tendencies, there is either the possibility of continuing to allude to classical and classical modernist architectural canons with the risk of knowingly playing the game of diminishing returns or the possibility of grasping the situation for its reformist potential.

Marcelo Villafañe's approach could be characterized as belonging to the latter category. How can the notion of the house be reformed to reconcile contemporary desires and tendencies, cultural conditions, realities, and facts? How can the reformist approach—one that acknowledges the spirit and the iconography of the idea of the house and at the same time wishes to re-embody both in a way that pays its respect to dense and ineradicable history without being entrapped by its charm—be true to its generators: clients, location, and culture? It can succeed if, as Villafañe has done, one takes a long, quiet, hard look at culture, location, and client. Working in Rosario, somewhat distanced from the busy-ness of the Argentinian capital, Villafañe has had the luxury of being the master of his time. From this position, a series of houses were designed, some built, that represent exactly this experiment: a language and approach that fits the stoic inhabitation of the vast countryside.

Suburban lifestyle in Argentina, as elsewhere, is as old as the city. With dense urban life arose the escapist desire to live closer to nature, in healthier surroundings. This basic motive has not changed over millennia; its ancient origins have spread across the globe via its modernized version in the Anglo-Saxon conception of the garden city. Here, in antiquity, lies the origin of the ideal-typical house: a double-pitched roof with a couple of windows and a front door.

In Argentina, this dream of life in the countryside is vital. Argentina is probably the one South American country, where a Western, not to say Euro-centric, culture has permeated almost all moments of everyday life among the dominant parts of the country's society. Few cultural signs of the indigenous people remain here, these having been successively displaced by the Incas, Mapuches, and Spanish descendants, the *criollos*. During the 20th-century, Europeans, in large part Spaniards and Italians, were attracted to the fertile country. The once truly affluent middle-class, which can still be seen wearing the Hispano-Italian interpretations of English dress codes in traditional restaurants in Buenos Aires such as *La Biela* or *Café Tortoni*—camel hair coats, navy blue cashmere sweaters, checkered Oxford shirts, corduroy trousers, pleated skirts—is steadfastly adhering to this dream of an additional life in the countryside.

Despite the economic crises that have engulfed Argentina in recent decades, or perhaps because of the social fallout from these, the mobile upper and middle-classes have commissioned houses, some weekend, some permanent, in newly designated, high-security residential estates. Concomitant with the widespread protests against the government and banks from 2001 to 2002, the few shops that were not already protected from irate protestors had roller shutters installed. Downtown Buenos Aires at night now appears as inhospitable as any other run-down, defensive city of the northern hemisphere. In an era of unregulated speculation, the causes for widespread, self-imposed, cultural impoverishment can be minute, the sense of social segregation immense.

And so houses, weekend or permanent, of the upper middle class are continuing to expand the edges of cities; this phenomenon has persisted since leisure, adequate pecuniary means, cheap land, and committed clients have existed. Add to these factors the mobility that comes with the car and one finds that houses of different sizes have been erected ever further from the cores of urban centers. For most architects, the critique of suburbia is by now almost second nature. The distension of infrastructure, the privatization of life, and the effect on the environment are commonly rehearsed issues. It is no less certain that the suburban model will lose its power in this part of the Americas any time soon—as in any other part of world—given the belated awareness of its cumulative effects on global climate. For that, the cultural footprint is still too deeply engrained here as elsewhere. Furthermore, from the profession's perspective, what architect would turn down a commission to design a house?

If anything, the majority of architects take up these commissions with enthusiasm. This building type continues to provide fertile ground for general as well as individual research, for the presentation of specific spatial and linguistic solutions, and for experiments in contemporary lifestyles.

The Florencia Raigal House is no exception in this context. Marcelo Villafañe had previously designed a house for Florencia's father, a club house for the estate, and subsequently a fourth house for another family within the same estate.

The Raigal Estate differs somewhat from more exclusive neighbors, where armed guards eye the visitor. Traditionally, the Raigal family has been devoted to horse riding, and Florencia regularly pursues her equestrian exercises beyond the weekends. Part of the building plot is fenced for her horses, which are otherwise sheltered in the nearby sheds of her father's house.

Located on the outskirts of Rosario, the site is part of the Pampas. Its characteristics are best experienced from one of the hundreds of privately operated buses that are the public transport system in this expansive country. Especially from the vantage point of the upper level of the double-decker buses and on clear days, the depth and breadth of view of the farmlands, with scattered trees and low hedges, reinforces the impression of infinite horizontal depth. There is no need for false perspectives here: distances are vast, real, and palpable. Trees in the foreground, those in the middle ground, and those in the distance create something of a measuring grid between the horizontal territory and recurring canopies. The domestication of one of the world's largest alluvial planes into tree- and hedge-denoted property subdivisions inhabited by a variety of herds and providing the soil for grains and wine, now increasingly includes the construction of single-family dwellings. These buildings occupy the subdivided flatlands in a way similar to the animals: lonesome solitaires that in their solitude accentuate the horizontal expanse of the Pampas. Unless the site already has vegetation, no new vegetation will be added in connection with the construction of new houses with some idea of landscape architectural design. It is the kind of direct or immediate relationship between building and surroundings that can also be found in the preparation of Argentina's staple diet of *parrillada* or *asados*: slabs of beef on the grill.

Florencia Raigal House, Marcelo Villafañe
Rosario, 2006

Seen over time, house designs on their own could, of course, provide a concise account of the development of architecture. But more significantly, what may be understood as a diachronic discourse—with houses ranging from Palladian and neo-Palladian, to modern and neo-modern—is nowadays also visible in any one of these estates, whether in Argentina or any other country, albeit constructed synchronically. Some estates are instant digests of architectural history.

The Florencia Raigal House can thus be understood as a purposefully calibrated instance of a free-standing house. Seen in the diachronic discourse, the house sets itself as a built critique of modernist phobias using modern construction logic, and as such, it is a thesis in the spatial development of the *oikos*.[1]

If to the modernist phobias could be counted the pitched roof, the unruly polygonal plan, the variety in compositional elements such as windows, and the non-orthogonal angle (the latter supposedly for reasons of the inefficient use of materials and unnecessary complexities in construction details), then the Florencia Raigal House asserts the possibility of "contravening" against all of these. With this house, Marcelo Villafañe has reached an ideal-typical status in his architectural search. Slinging a polygonal roof with a clear ridge line over a series of volumes is no simple feat. Certainly, the formal freedom of allowing volumes to extend beyond a self-

1. *Oikos*, the ancient Greek word for house or household, was often considered the cornerstone of ancient Greek society.

imposed corset of a single and simple geometric configuration may render the problem of roofing such a rambling composition more easy. In fact, the compositional control required to stretch a polygonal roof over a seeming rambling design requires precise spatial imagination, which is exactly the impulse that is giving rise to the house in its totality.

Marcelo Villafañe is a virtuoso when it comes to understanding buildings in their sculptural, figural dimension. Not unlike a tailor, who imagines the extent to which two-dimensional fabric is cut and sewn so as to accompany, even enhance, the shape of the body inhabiting it, Villafañe experiments with the folding and plying of surfaces to create both an outline and ridgeline, as well as distinct internal spaces.

The polygonal roof shape is based on the flattened skin of a cow, the hide, as it is wondrously spread-eagled from the complex, three-dimensional, physical being into a perfectly two-dimensional plane. To some extent, Villafañe's experiments in house roof forms returns this two-dimensional motif to oversized three-dimensional figures in the Pampas. If the cow leather–lined BKF chair offers a concave receptacle for an individual, then Villafañe's adaptations and transformations of the cowhide motif become family-sized shelters.[2] At one level of the discourse then, the homage to the hide is a celebration of a core component of Argentinean culture.

Rather than being just a loose assembly of spaces and forms with a dubious double-pitched roof, the Florencia Raigal House marks the culmination of a serious line of built research in the application of the cowhide motif.

If for classical and neo-classical architecture the orders as motifs and the modules as the proportional disciplining device were the departure point for both simple and complex structures, and if for academic modernism the inversion of all matters classical gave rise to a composed dynamism through plastic asymmetry, a longing for objects lifting off the ground, and uninterrupted views from the building especially at the building's corner, then Villafañe's "invention" of the cowhide motif is equal to any abstract ordering discipline found in the history of architecture.

The importance in such an "invention," whether personal or subsequently more widely shared, is the potential for such a device to engage multitudes of compositional challenges. Besides achieving an adequate balance in the cowhide's literal or vestigial presence, thereby demonstrating the precise control over the degree of ambiguity that this motif requires, the application of the motif fulfils basic expectations in that the house's ridge line marks the "spine;" internally, the steel beams create the "ribbing" of the roof structure, these steel beams in turn being connected by composite plywood open box joists, as a continuation of the plywood soffit, analogous to tendons and muscles.

The Florencia Raigal House is far from Jean-Jaques Lequeu's literal oversized cowshed in the shape of a cow. It is far from the magnified puppy dogs of late-20th-century artists. Yet, it is another liberating step away from the narrow-minded concept of house-ness of late modernism seen in the hundreds of orthogonal boxes that populate suburban Europe, as well as a courageous tightrope walk toward the archetypal image of a house. Villafañe's house stands in line with the liberating research conducted by such architects as Josef Frank (his house designs for Dagmar Grill from 1947) or Knut Knutsen (his summer house at Portør, Norway, of the same period). Here were two architects willing to step outside the formal constraints of functionalism and into experimentation with geometrically unrestrained configurations and spatial planning. For Knutsen (in his summer house project and

2. The BKF chair was designed by the Argentinian architect Jorge Ferrari Hardoy in 1938 while working for the Austral Group in Buenos Aires. His partners, Antonio Bonet and Juan Kurchan, were also part of the Austral Group, hence the chair was named "BKF".

later in an unbuilt project [1961] for an extension to the Villa Edstrand by Sigurd Lewerentz), there is more than the configurational reverberation of the inner volumes: the building as such takes on a life of its own, an animation beyond the logic of form, one that cannot be all that easily controlled, as Alvaro Siza, another architect willing to engage in the design of buildings as figures, not merely as the mechanical embodiment of an internal metric, has also observed.

If the modernist tried to disclaim any such basis for the design of form, it is architects such as Marcelo Villafañe who are recuperating the expressive dimension of a building's configuration, while at the same time grounding every component of the building in a visceral logic.

The two-story Florencia Raigal House is composed along the cowhide motif into a set of four splayed volumes; these, in turn, are differentiated into one narrower and one wider pair. Facing the estate's access road is the narrower pair of spaces, containing the utilities and a small bedroom and veiled by an open weave blockwork wall. Looking toward the yet unsettled east is the wider set of spaces complete with the covered terrace, the double height living space, and the master bedroom

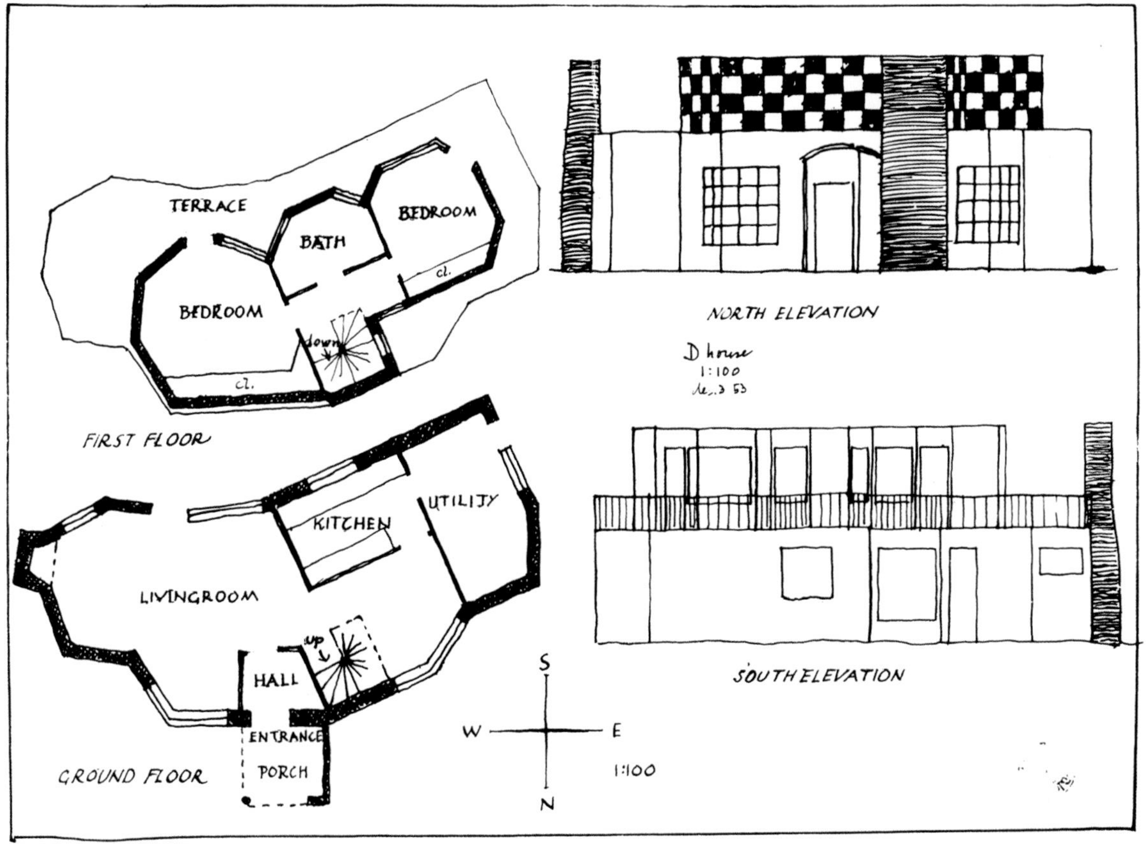

Dagmar Grill, Josef Frank
unbuilt, 1953

on the upper floor. A large landing serves as an office gallery, overlooking the living room. The internal atmosphere of the house is relaxed, the spaces at ease with the site and their outer form.

What can be sensed through the shroud-like west façade—the house's orientation toward the more private east—is partly experienced in the

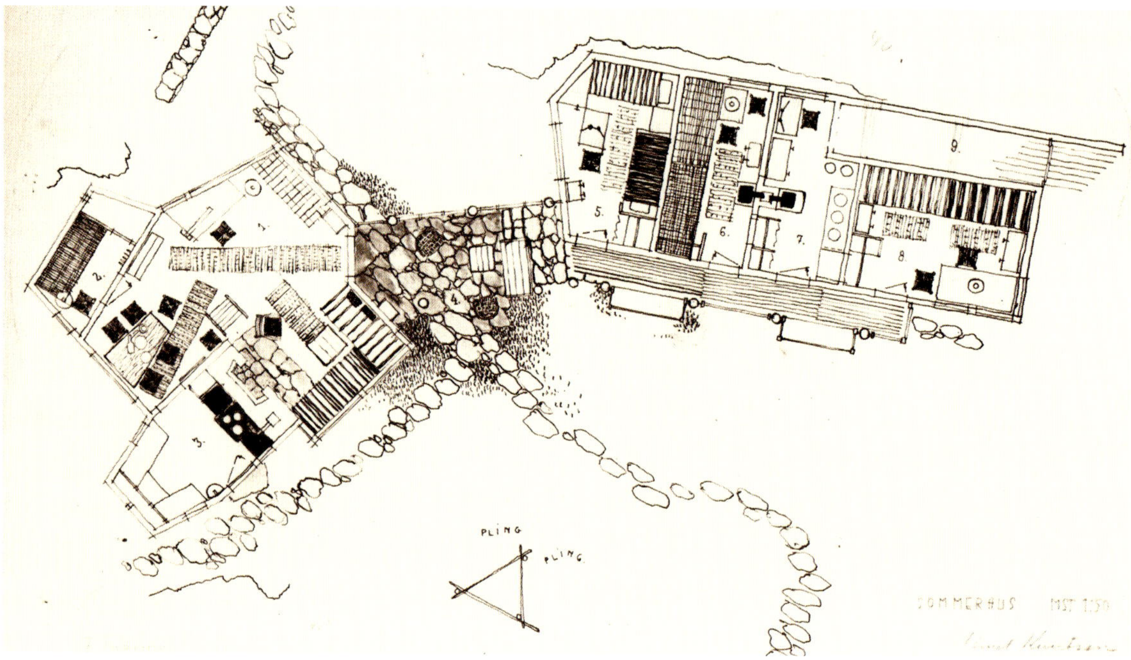

Summerhouse, Kunt Knutsen, elevation sketch and plan
Portør, built 1949

access to the house. The main door is located in the acute angle of the south-facing quasi court. The visitor thus approaches along two sharply pointed blank walls in order to face away from the main spaces upon entering the house. On turning at the quasi vestibule, which doubles as the sitting area in front of the kitchen counter, the visitor stands at the crossing point between the four wings. From here, much of the house is disclosed: differentiated uses are indicated by the type of openings in the single skin, load-bearing, concrete block wall.

In a self-evident way, the extremities of the four wings are something between grand bay windows and objectified/externalized rooms. The staircase then logically occupies the double height volume to land at the center of the upper level.

Internally, the views, as framed by the walls, are laid out in such a way as to maximize the spatial experience of the interior. Thus the house's self-sufficiency is established; within the expanse of the Pampas, the raw cruciform, the "X" marking the site, and the internal spatial crossing pins down the artifice's locus.

The idea of the cross, the X, has occupied Villafañe for some time, beginning with a

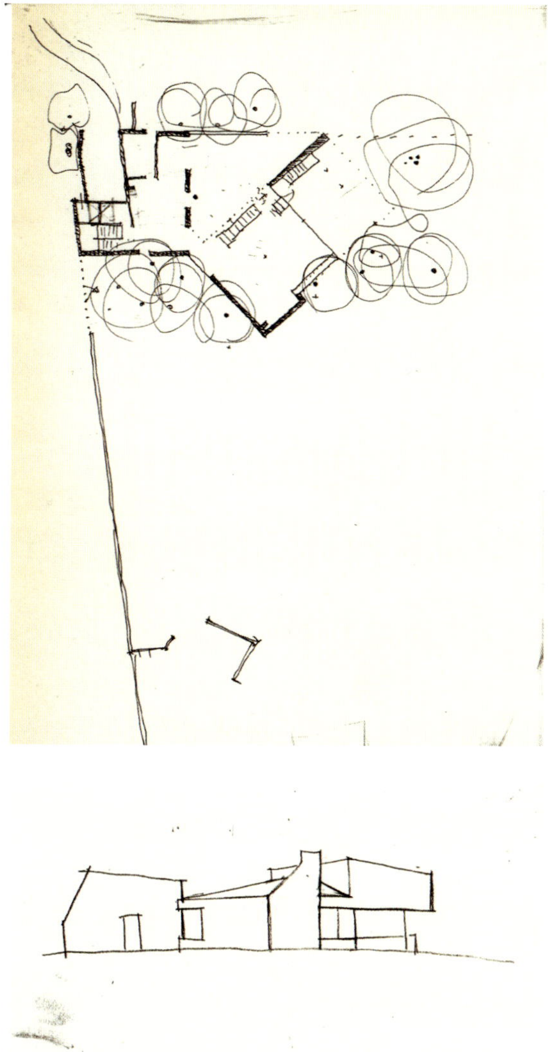

Villa Edstand, Sigurd Lewerentz, plan, elevation and perspective sketch 1961, Swedish Architecture Museum

constructional concept for lattice work that later was extended into the creation of a series of steps for a staircase. The gluing of double-square plywood rectangles in a zigzag arrangement constitutes the risers and runs of a stair. (In its earlier version at the Casa Brown, this constructional system was applied in a massive, solid way; here at the Florencia Raigal House the construction is pared down to a structural minimum.)

In the same way, the lattice-like windows facing the road, created by the open jointing of the otherwise stack-bonded blockwork, are the obverse of the staircase construction: the one a criss-crossing of space, devoid of structural integrity, and the other constituting a structural bond. In the two acute "courtyards," paired windows follow this compositional motif. One can thus recognize the transposition of a constructional idea via a motif from its origin in the staircase (material construction) to the blockwork and wall construction (window voids) and the cowhide (formal motif) to the spatial concept of the house.

The Florencia Raigal House stands for an external formal expression synthesizing internal volumes. This may not sound like a great achievement and, in the context of relatively simple building codes that are able to ignore the effects of cold-bridges (i.e., in a context that does not require the separation of internal layers from the external layers), the constructional details can be direct and light throughout. Thus window frames are simple metal profiles; the wall is a single layer of blockwork; and the roof consists of a water-proofing membrane and a layer of reinforced plywood. However, what makes this house significant, over and above other houses by Villafañe with similar underlying notions (e.g., Casa Brown) and over above houses by other architects, is the fact that this house is the essence of a configured set of spaces. The house's succinctness is achieved by the relative flushness of surfaces and the absence of drip mouldings or ledge overhangs (see particularly the edges of the roof).

Distinct from the orthogonal, modular, trabeated Hellenistic tradition, and distinct too from the a-constructive looseness of modernist neo-plasticism, the Florencia Raigal House reveals an architecture that is sculptural while being rooted in real construction and that is succinctly spatial at the same time as this spatiality is re-presented on its sculptural exterior. It brings to the point the nuanced freedom of the inflection, whether it is an inflection from the orthogonal or parallel or from the vertical or horizontal. With this nuanced freedom, the house marks an edge toward the road and opens itself to the Pampas beyond. It marks the spot in the landscape by its quasi cruciform. It extends itself outwards via the same cruciform wings. While the wings are allowed to spread, they are gathered underneath the one splayed roof, which rises to a central ridge asserting the house's unity.

Inevitably, it is always possible to regard any building as embodying, in one aspect or another, vestiges of other buildings or traditions. Thus it could be argued that the Florencia Raigal House embodies a vestige of, for example, the Fisher House (1960) by Louis Kahn in terms of the geometric shift, or the Venna Venturi House (1962) by Robert Venturi in terms of the condensed spatial typology, or even looking further back into architectural history, a vestige of the Villa Capra (ca. 1567–71) by Andrea Palladio. But now, in the Florencia Raigal House, the wings having been transformed through a functional lens into specific uses and only the two slim steel posts outside the ground floor living room represent the true vestige of the Palladian portico.

However, such references simultaneously reveal the specificity of the Florencia Raigal House. It is more specific to the site than evident from the aerial views or at first glance. It is structured coherently on the basis of the crossing spaces and the splayed wings. It has an internal motivation. In other words, it is more itself, more an individual contribution to the architectural discourse than any vestige of previous instances. More importantly, in the context of the architectural discourse, the house is unselfconsciously assertive and faithfully relaxed. It is a house as an inherent manifestation, not one in need of a manifesto.

Raigal House
Marcelo Villafañe

The house is positioned to generate an anti-mimetic relationship with the site. With its panoramic views of the landscape, the observer registers a vast and flat topography. Clearly, the house is settled on the Pampas.[1]

It is a two story house: bedrooms upstairs with a double-height space and living area in back. The building is composed of a cross-shaped plan that generates different types of angles, some of them very acute, yet always unrestricted and free in their movement.

When approaching the house, the entrance is not seen at first glance; the visitor has to look for it as part of the experience. The main door is found by walking around the house, placed in the vertex of the more acute of the angles generated by the two volumes. From the approach, the house seems to be turning its back, with a large, perforated wall as the main facade. It is here in this wall, that the kitchen and utility rooms are located, giving more privacy to the living areas, as well as direct contact with the backyard and the Pampas beyond.

1. An extensive, treeless grassland area found in southern South America, especially in Argentina.

The multiple faces of the perimeter display both clear and dark shadows that vary according to the hour of the day and position of the sun. Diagonally cast shadows can be seen on some of its faces, helping to further disarticulate the shape of the house.

The concept of system goes along with any logical thinking; it is a support structure. The repetition of concrete blocks generates a constructive system that allows for the absence of elements—these holes become colored glass windows; while some can be opened, some are fixed, and others reveal themselves to be only recessed blocks.

The staircase is composed of a five-plywood-piece system. Horizontal boards work as treads but also provide the only lateral stability. The separation between the structural components allows for an unstable sensation that it is merely an illusion.

This idea of working between a systematic order and a broken grid—logical thinking with chaotic variations—results in a new order: one freer, less formal, and more amorphous, and something I am more comfortable with these days, work after work.

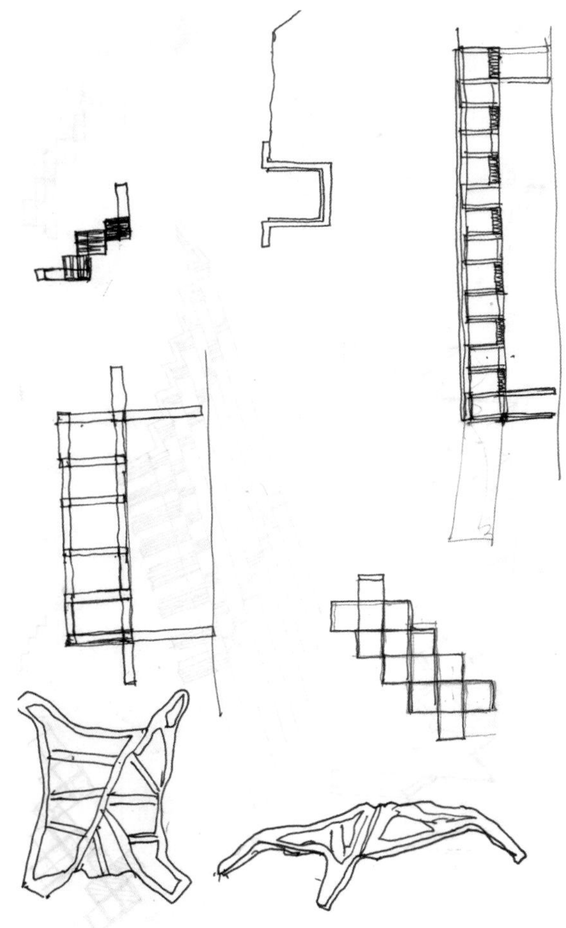

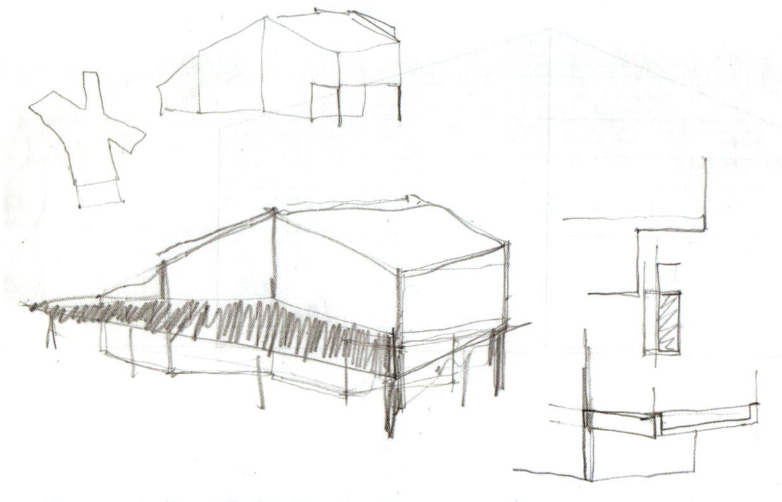

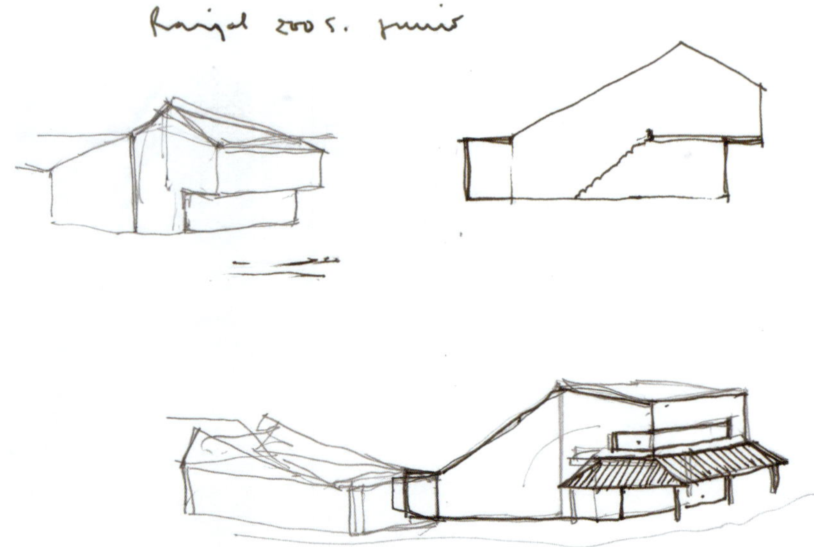

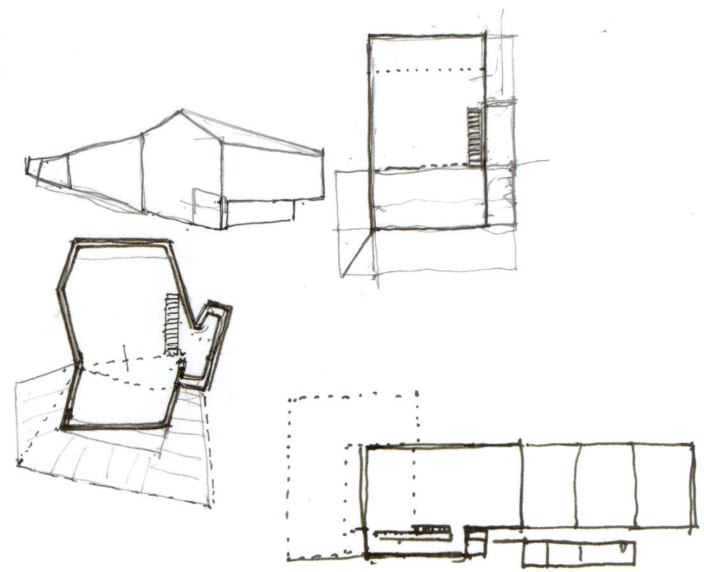

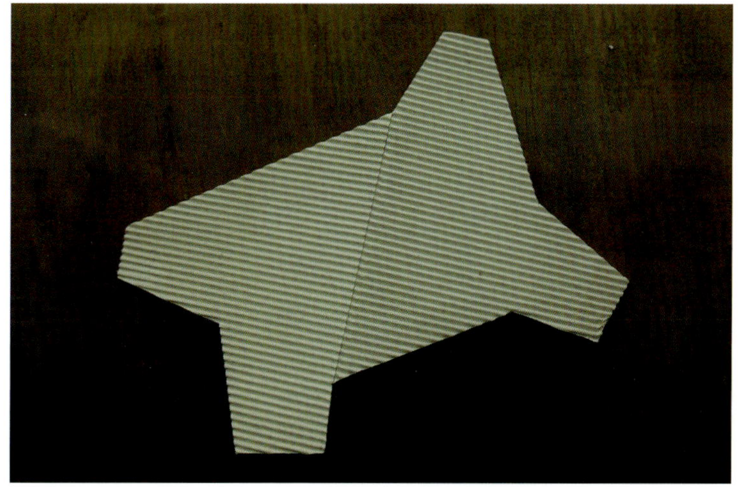

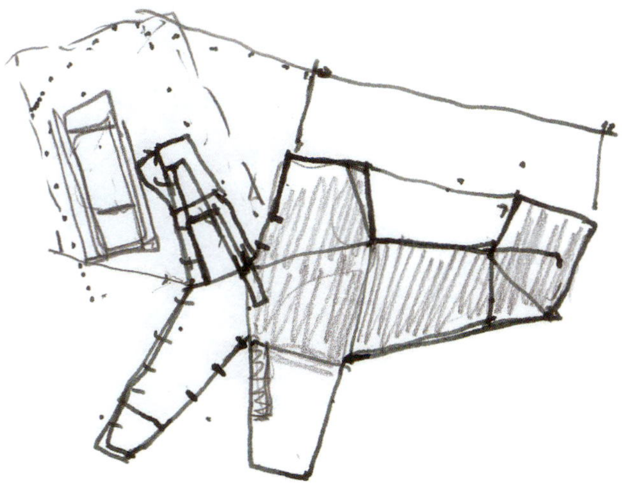

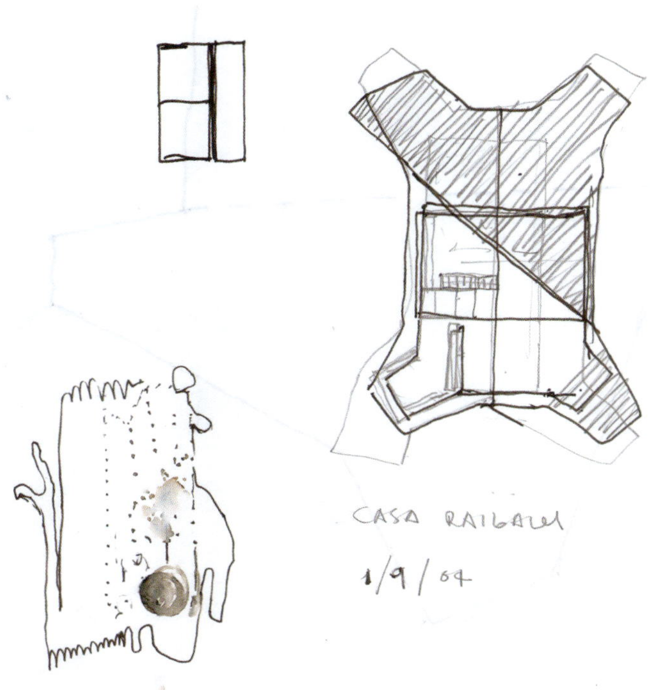

93

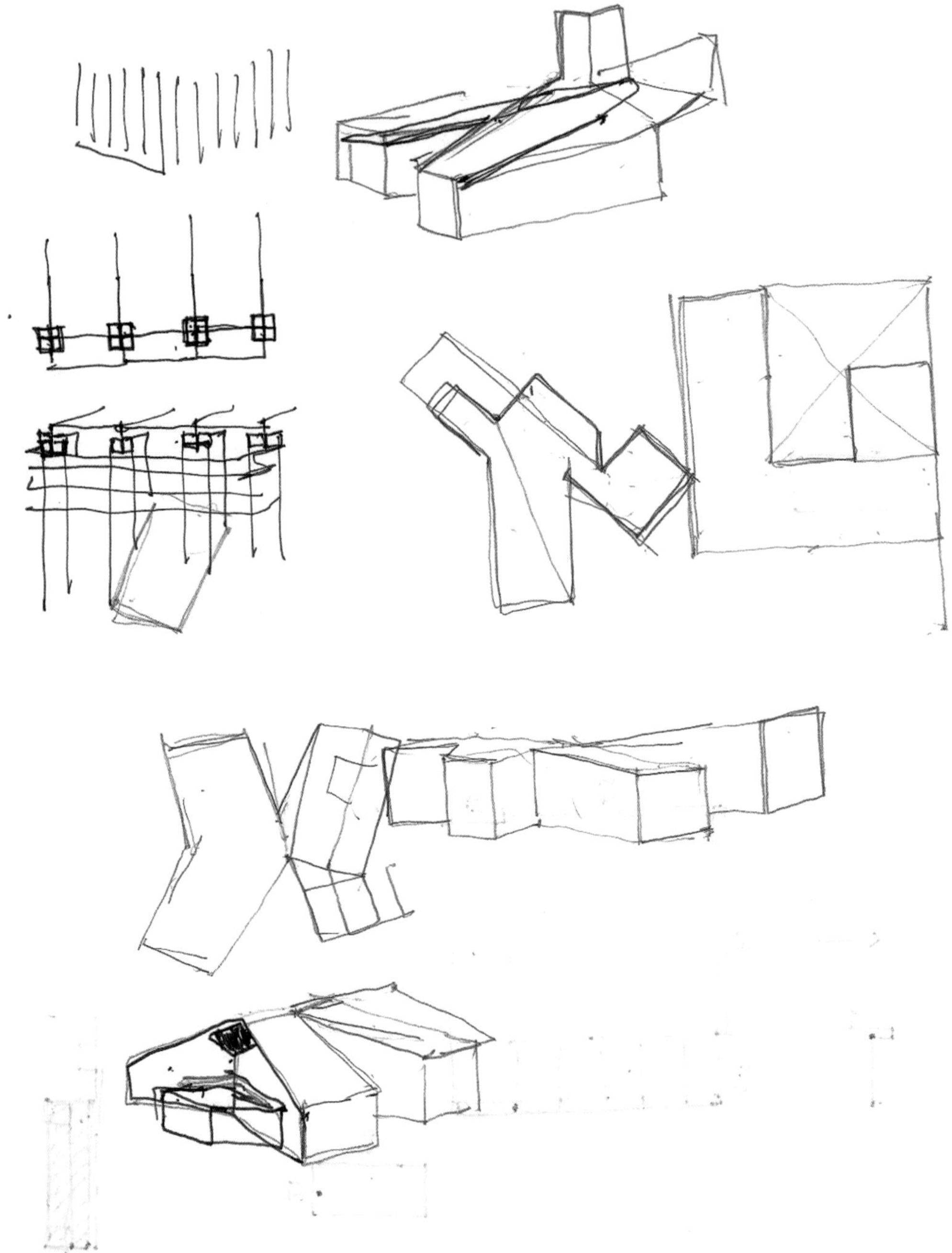

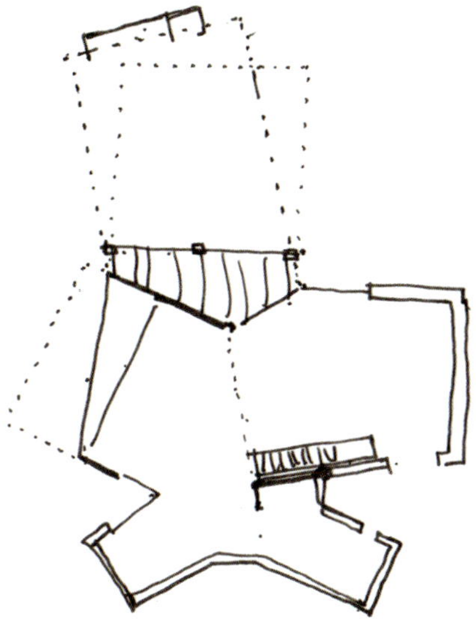

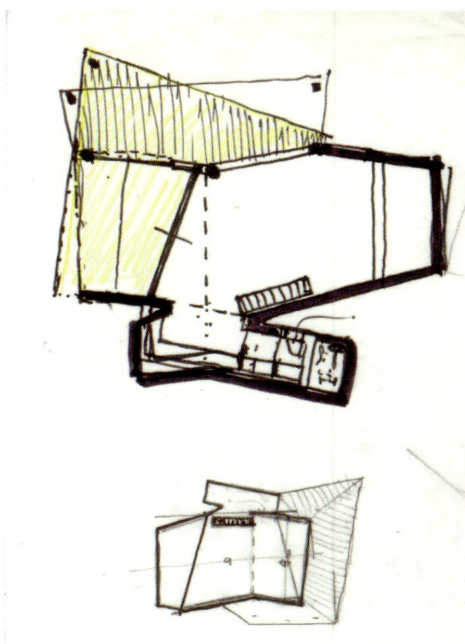

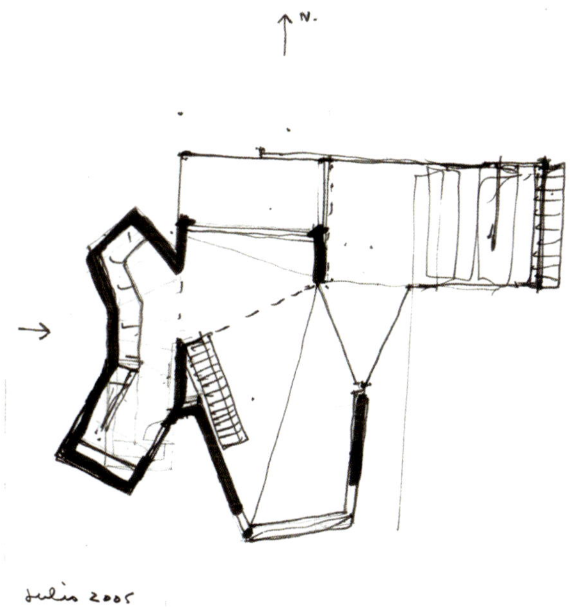
N.
Julio 2005

1/125

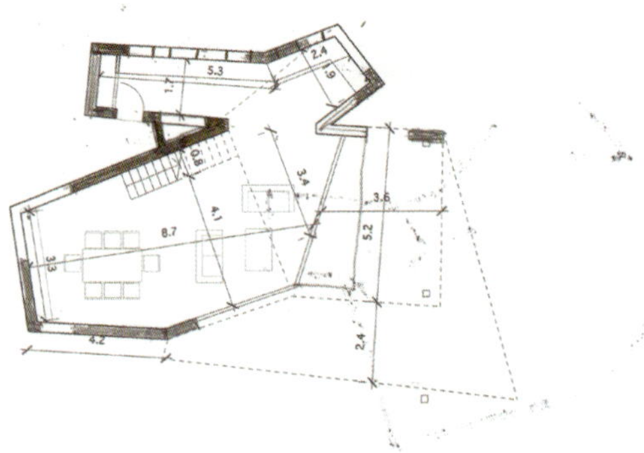

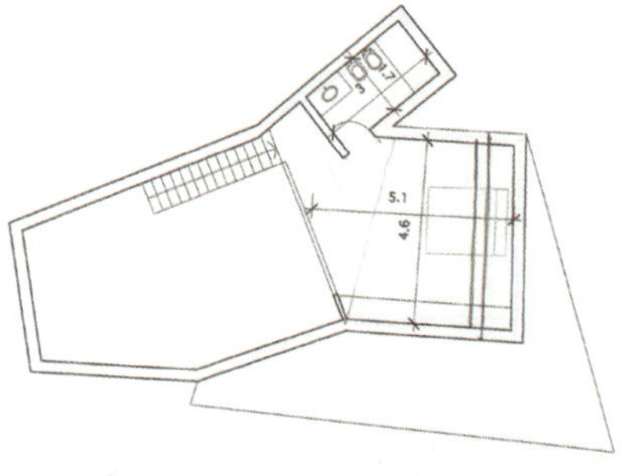

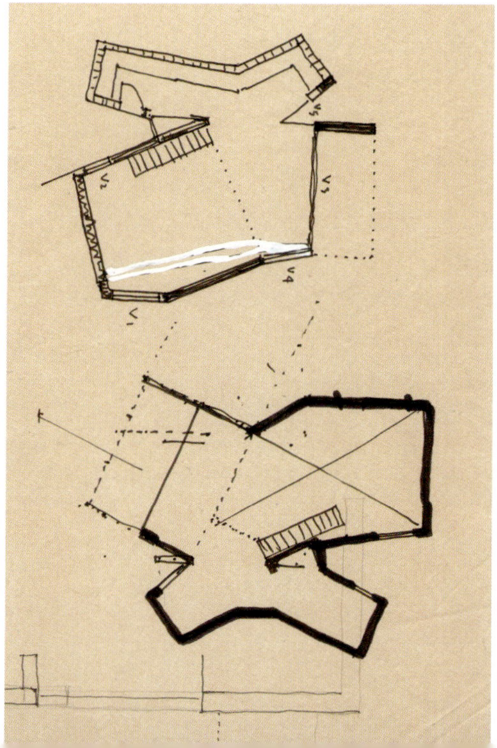

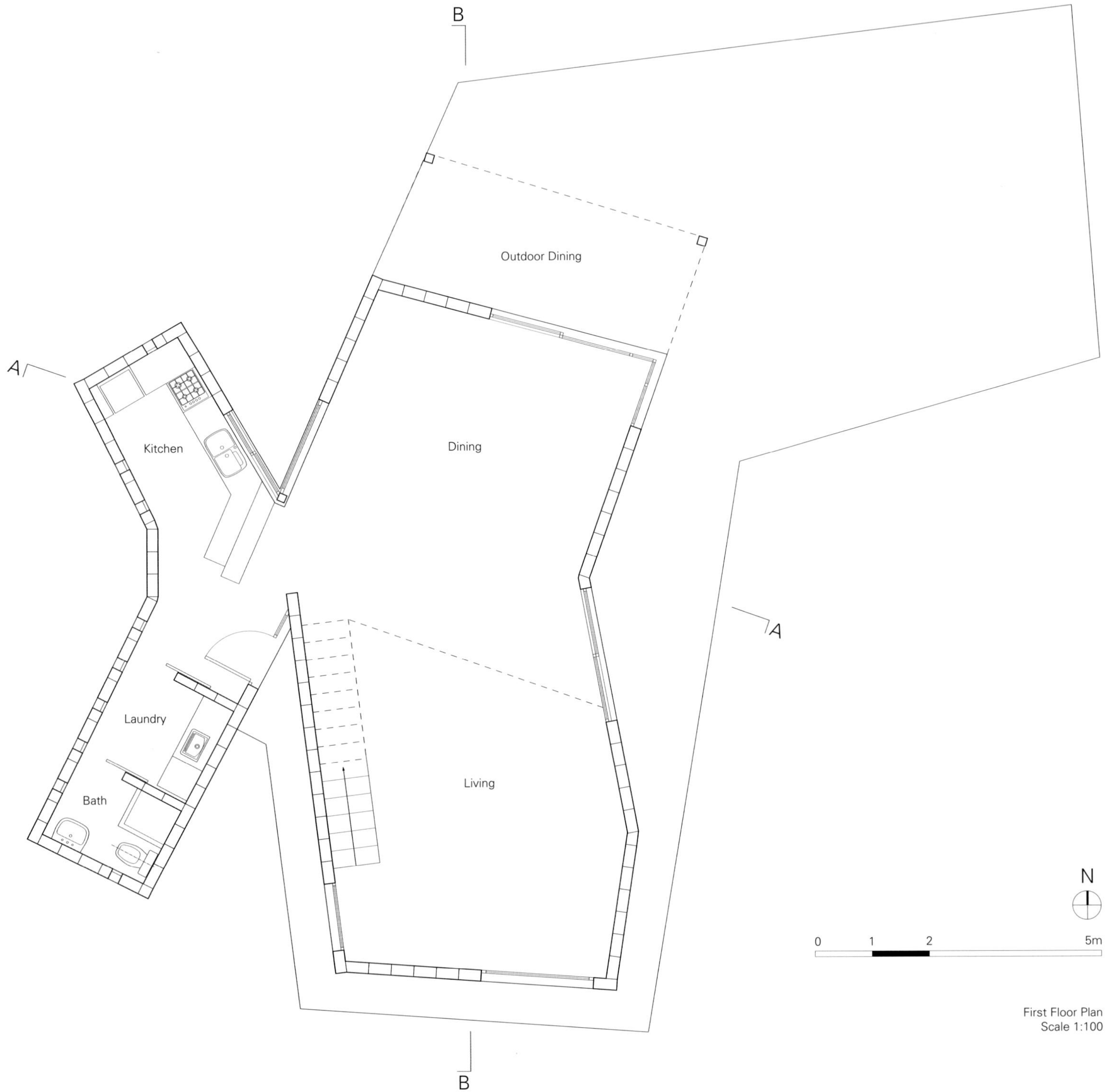

First Floor Plan
Scale 1:100

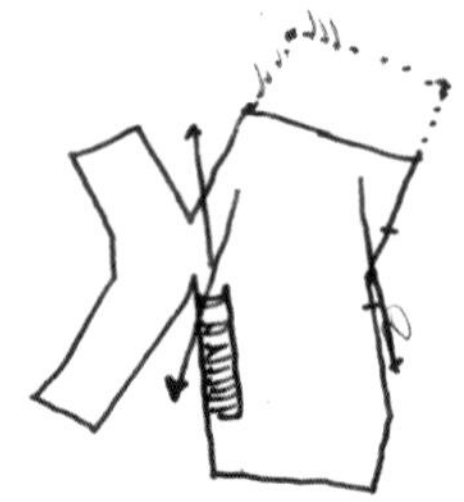

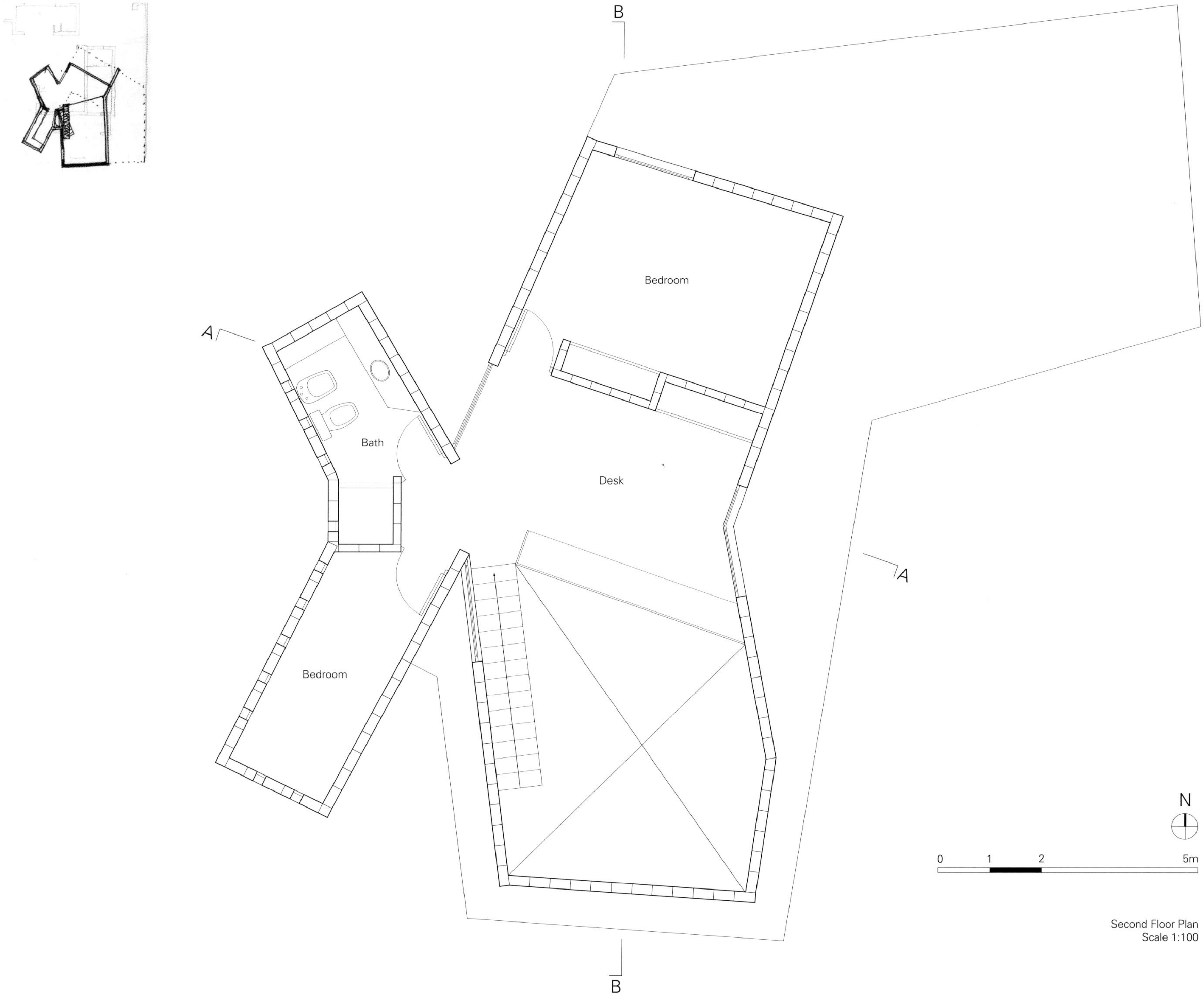

Second Floor Plan
Scale 1:100

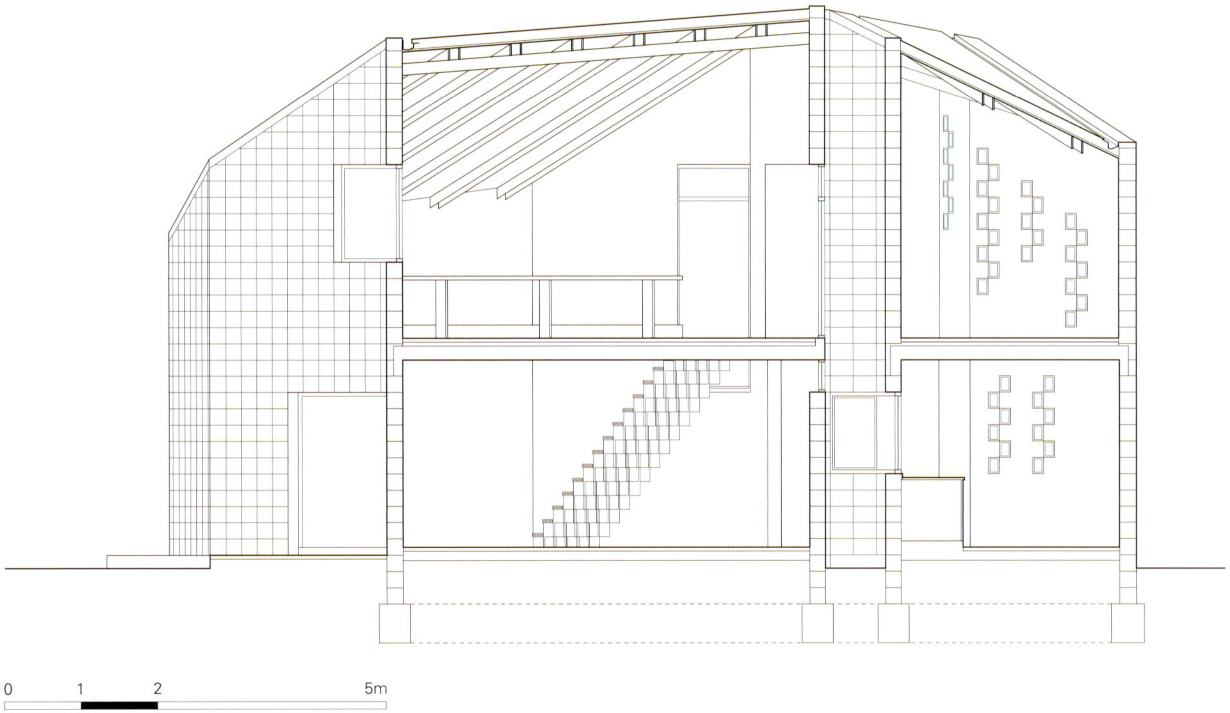

Section A – A
Scale 1 : 100

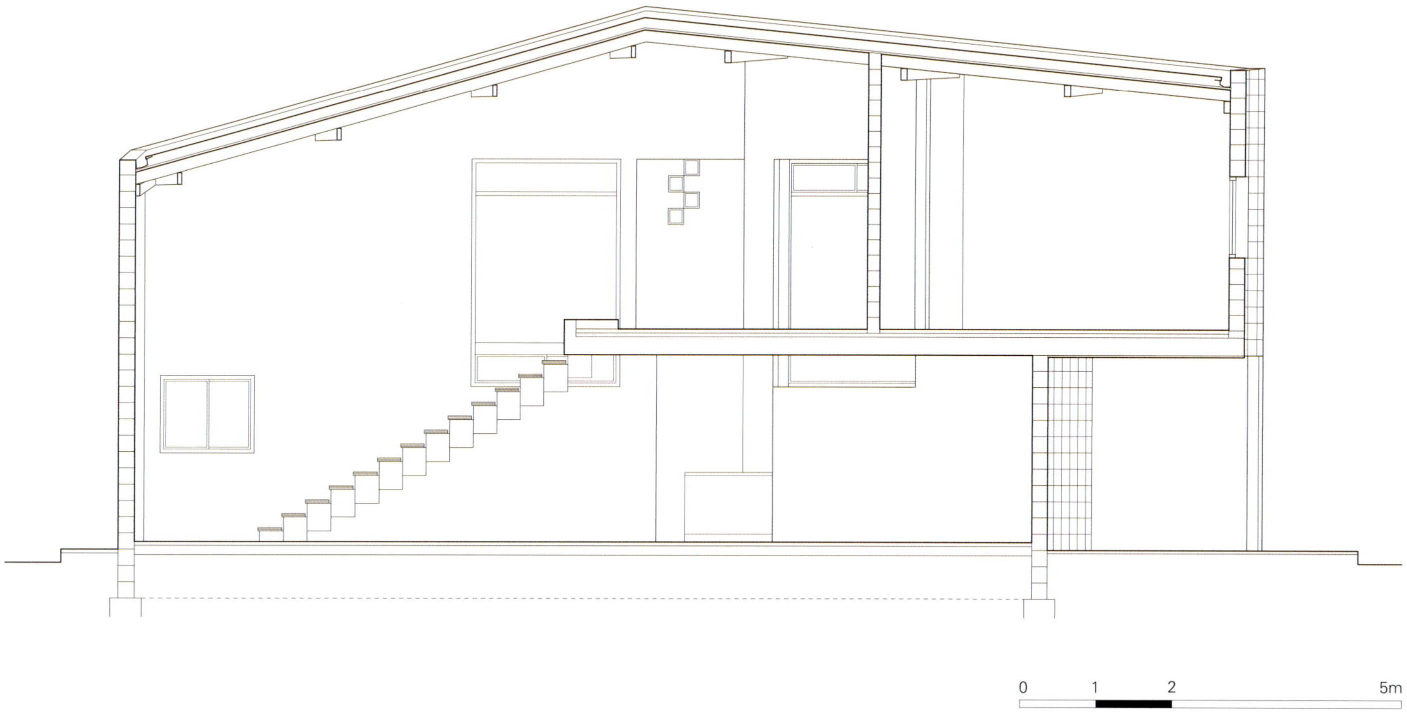

Section B – B
Scale 1 : 100

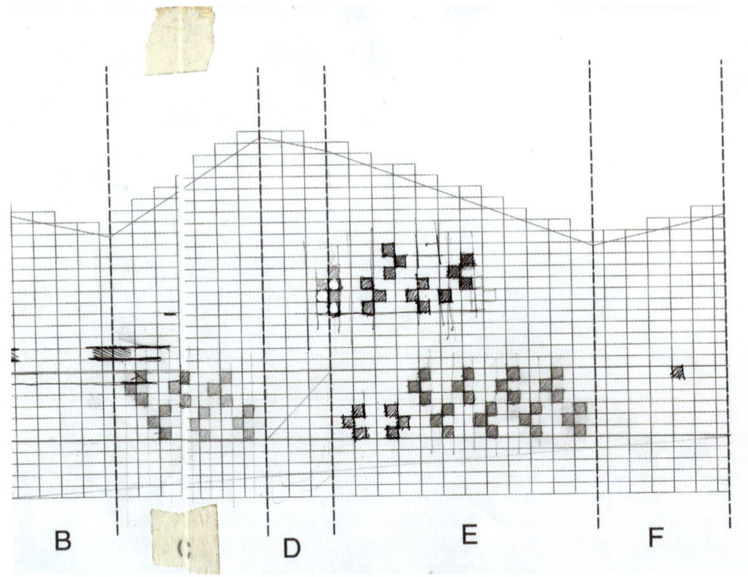

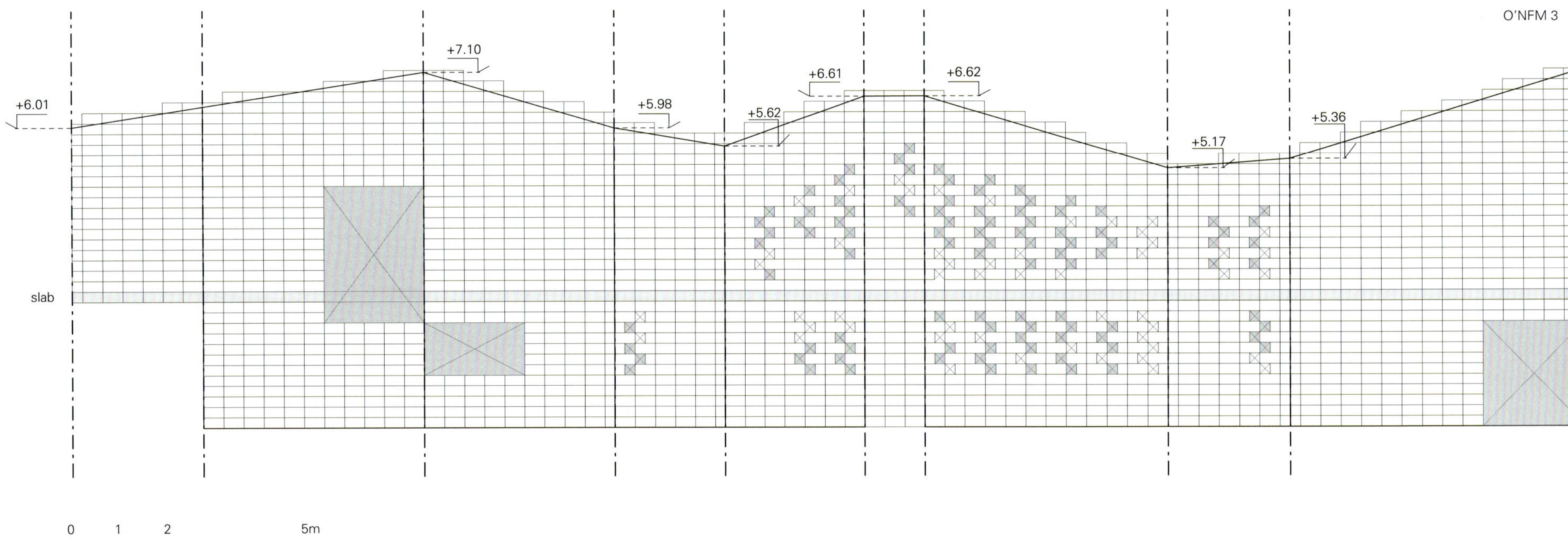

Elevation Study
Scale 1 : 125

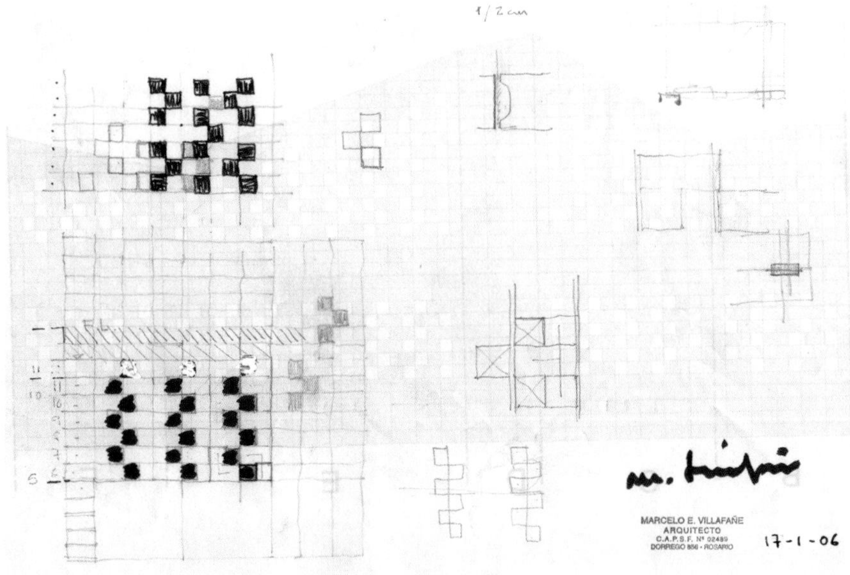
1/2 cm
MARCELO E. VILLAFAÑE
ARQUITECTO
17-1-06

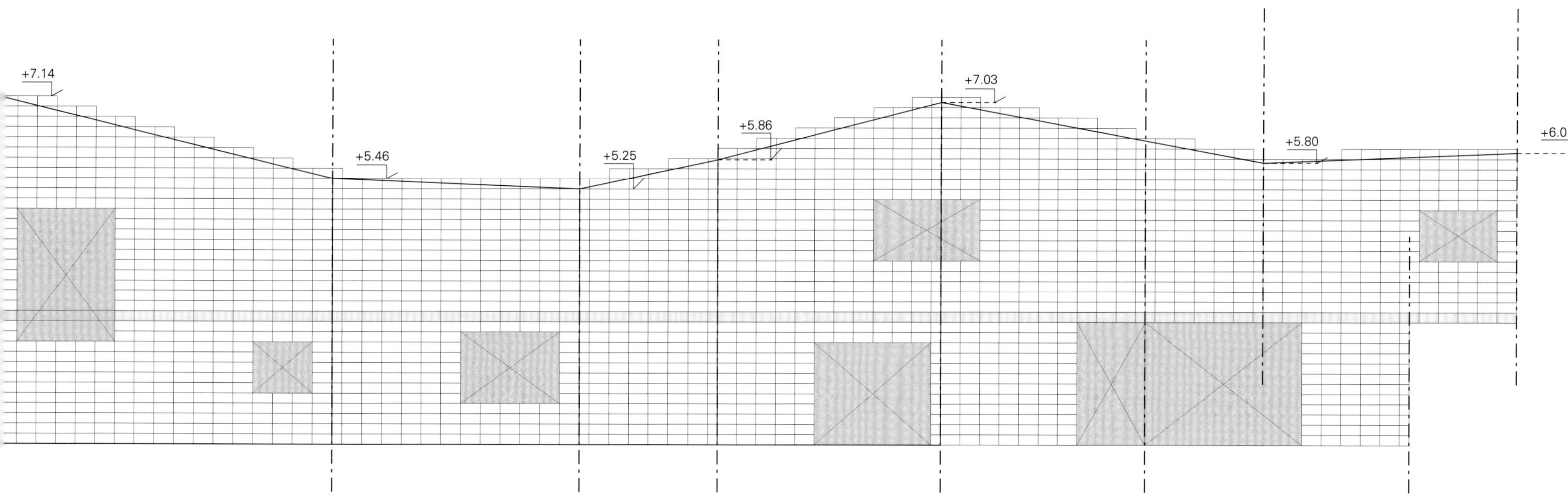
+7.14
+5.46
+5.25
+5.86
+7.03
+5.80
+6.01

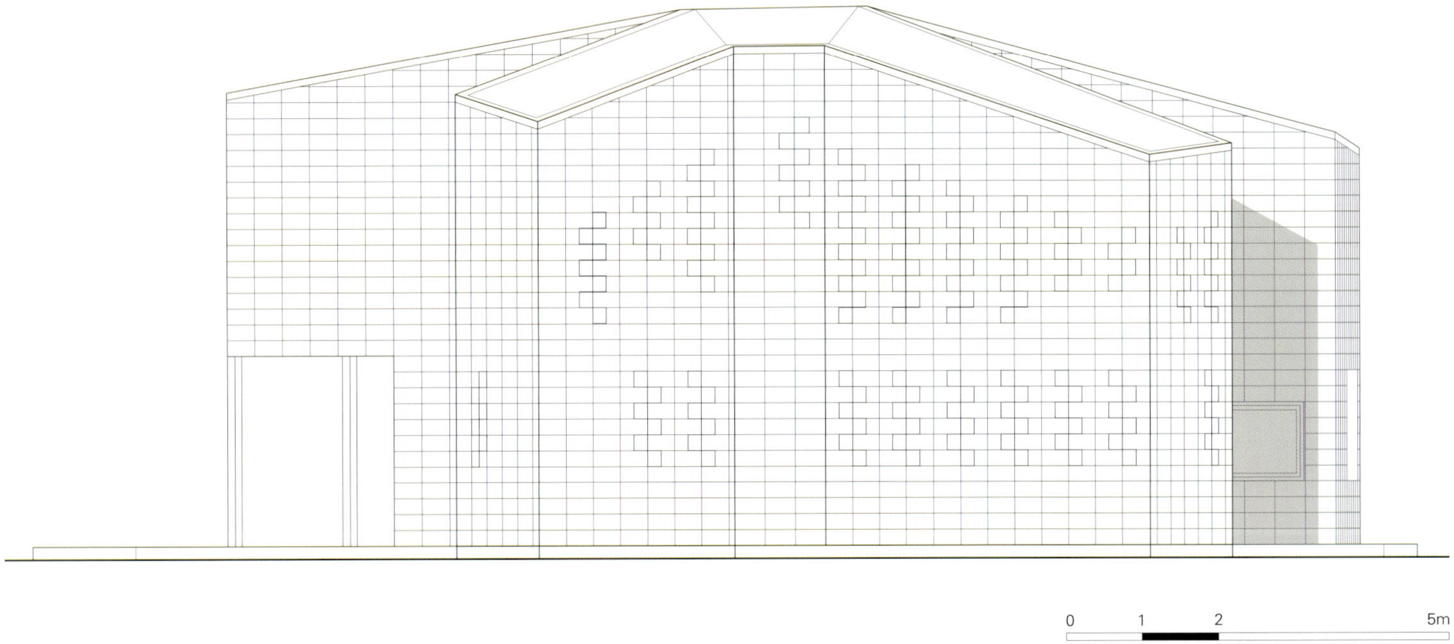

West Elevation
Scale 1 : 100

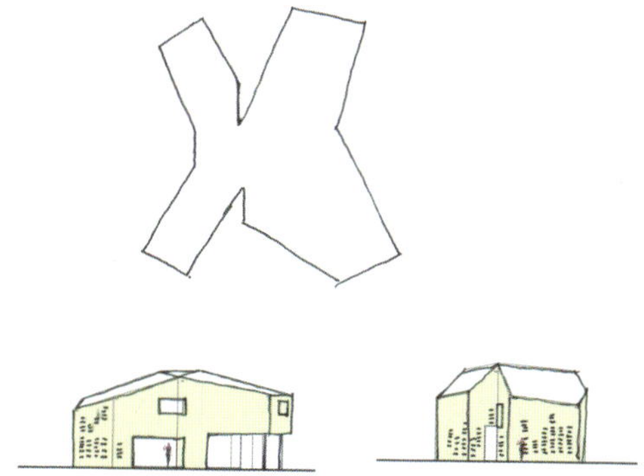

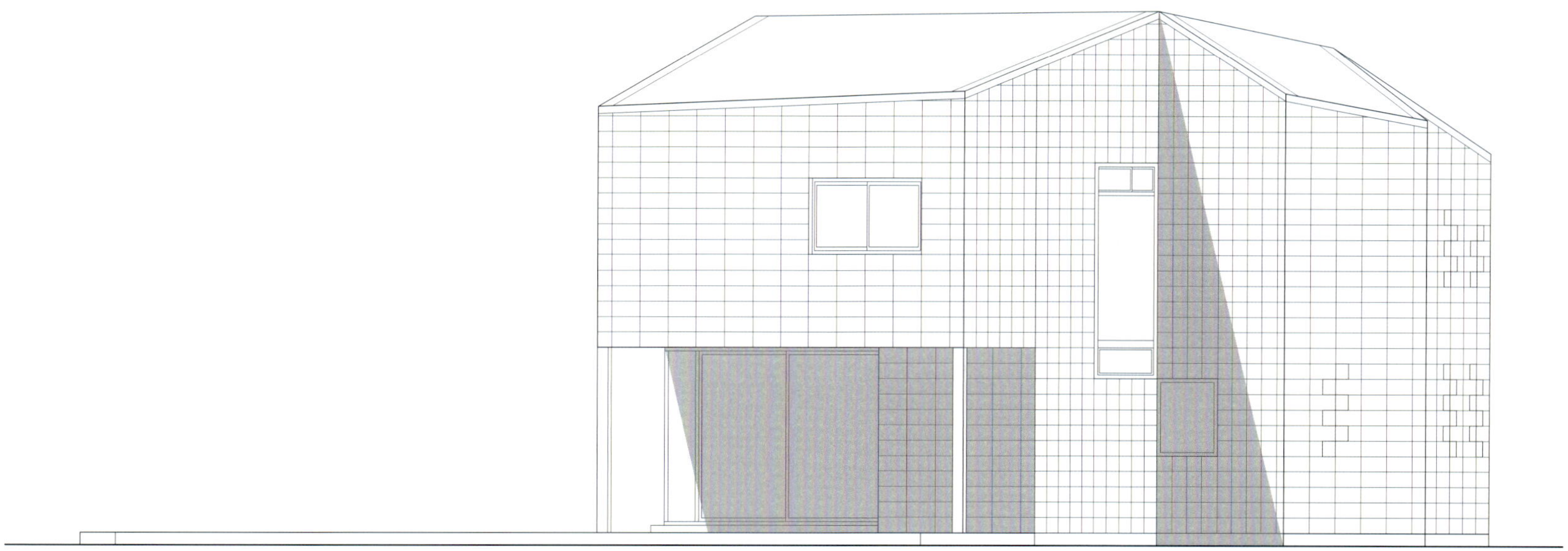

0 1 2 5m

North Elevation
Scale 1 : 100

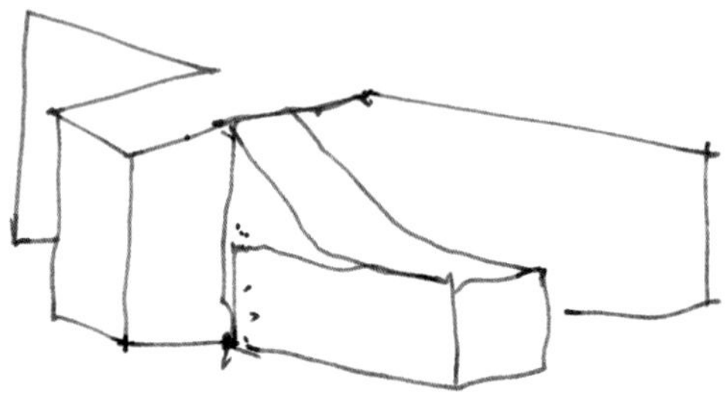

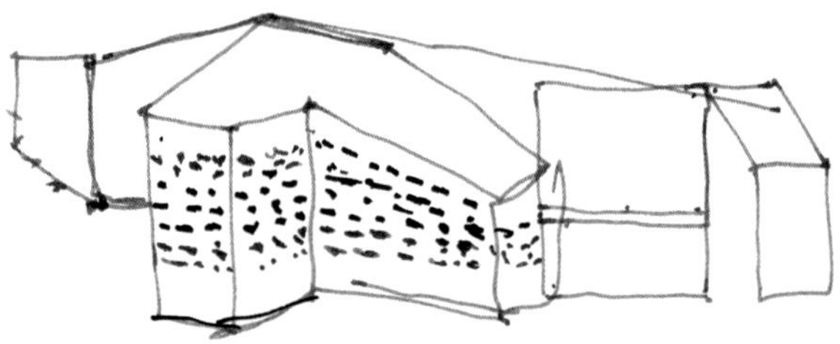

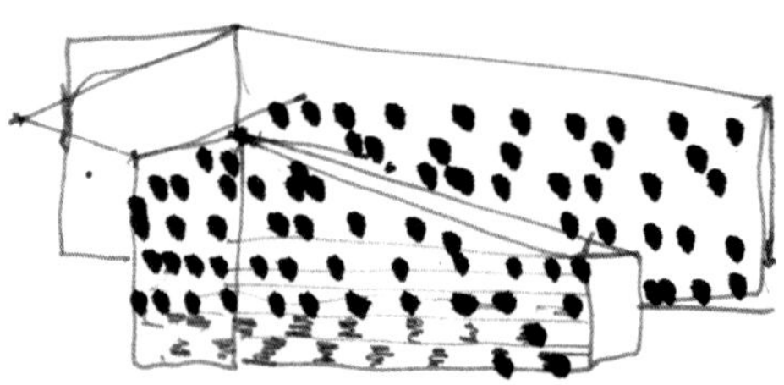

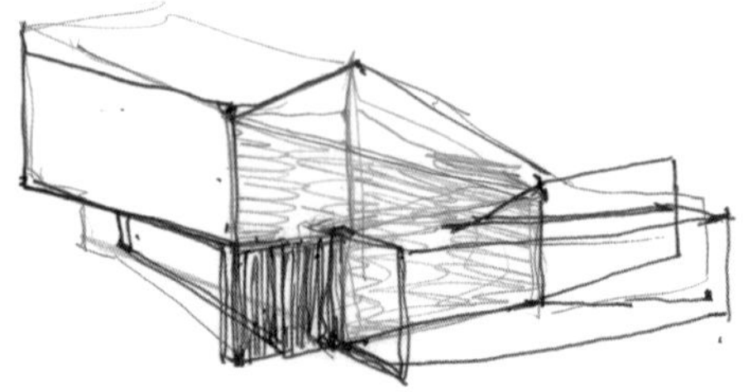

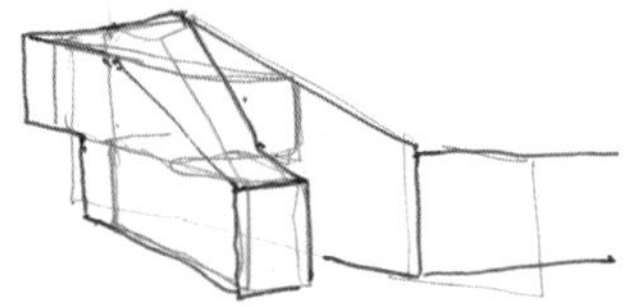

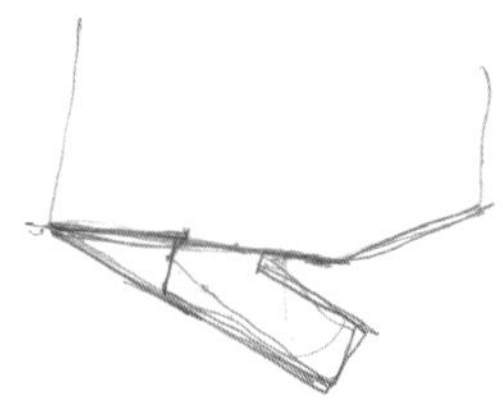

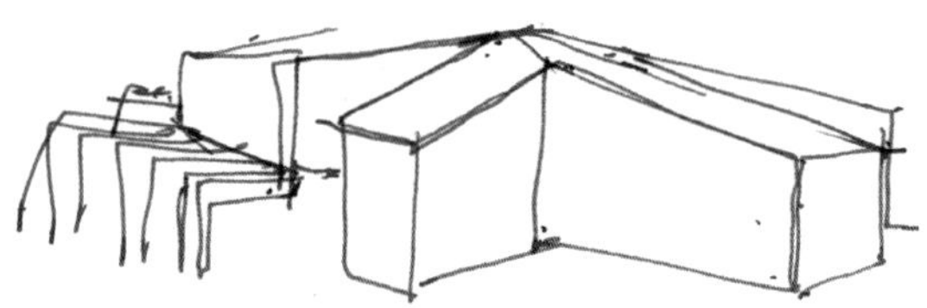

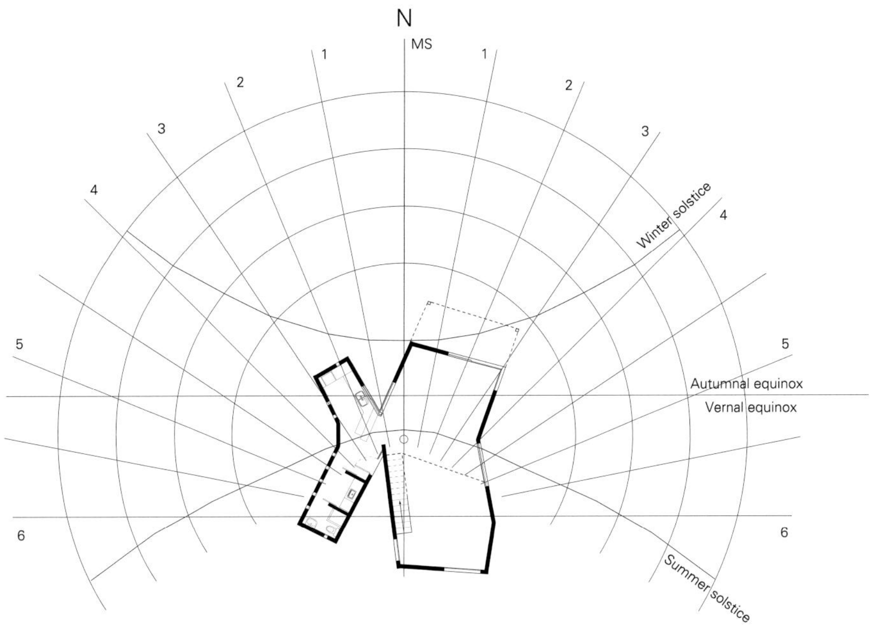

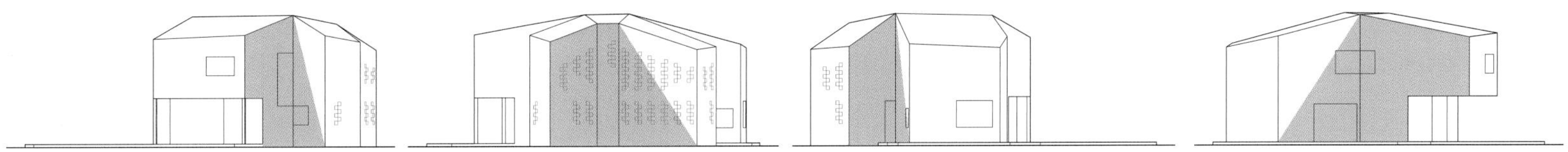

Shadow Study Diagram
Not to Scale

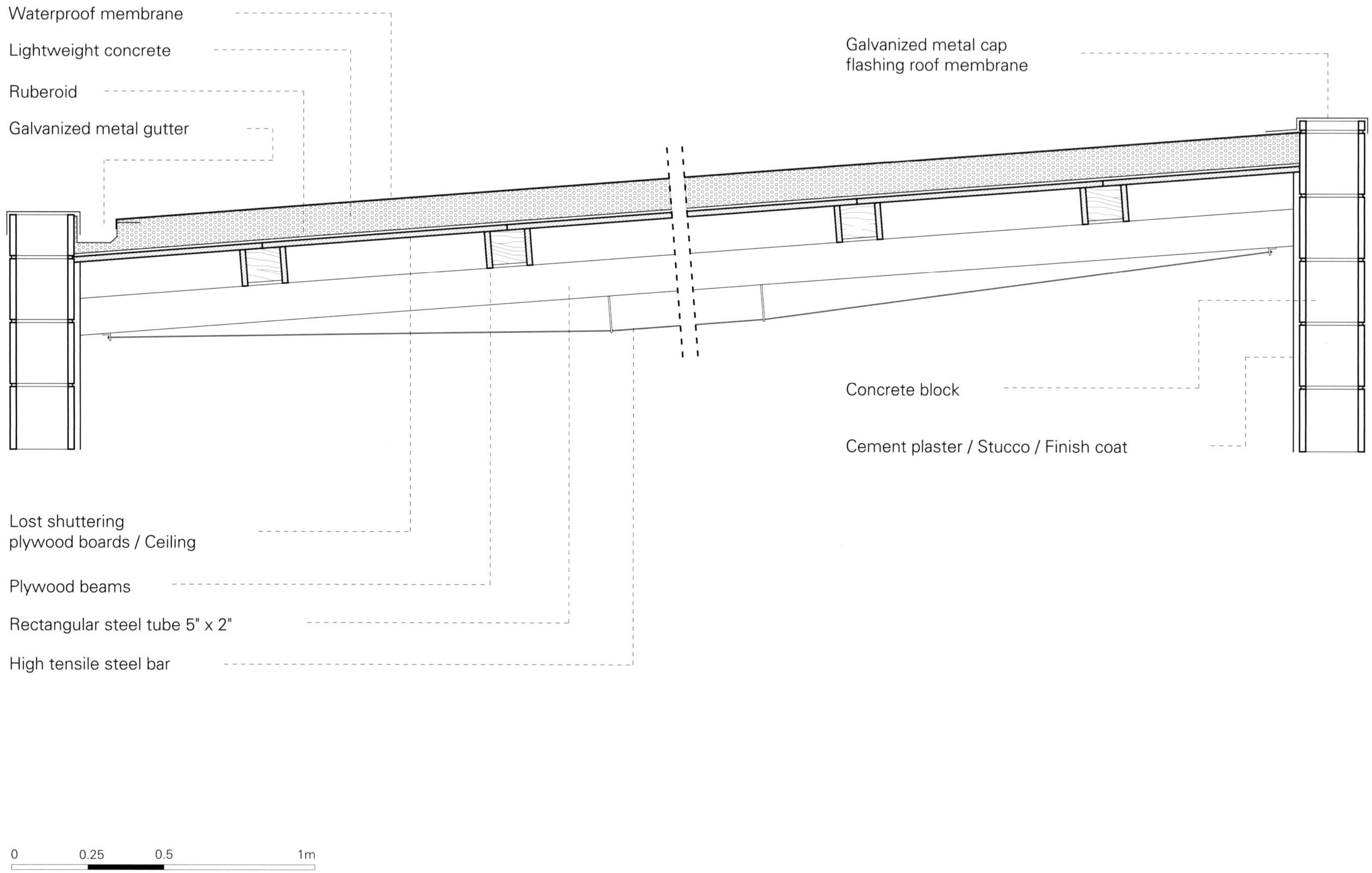

Roof Assembly Detal
Scale 1 : 20

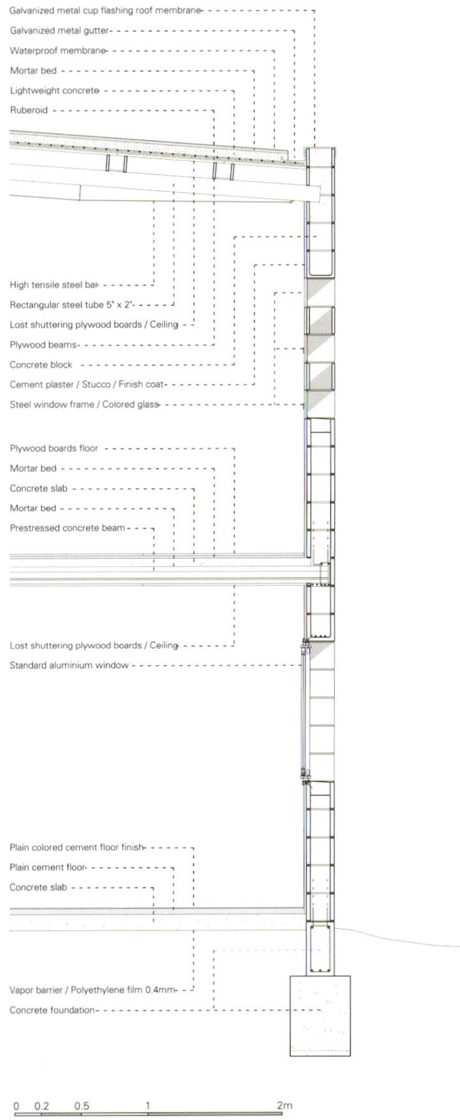

Wall Section

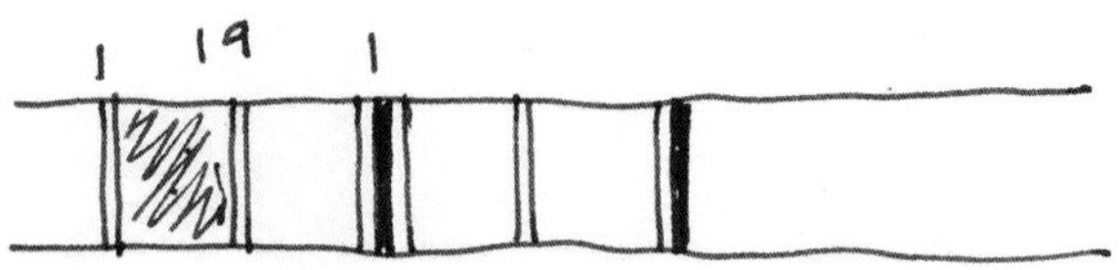
1 19 1

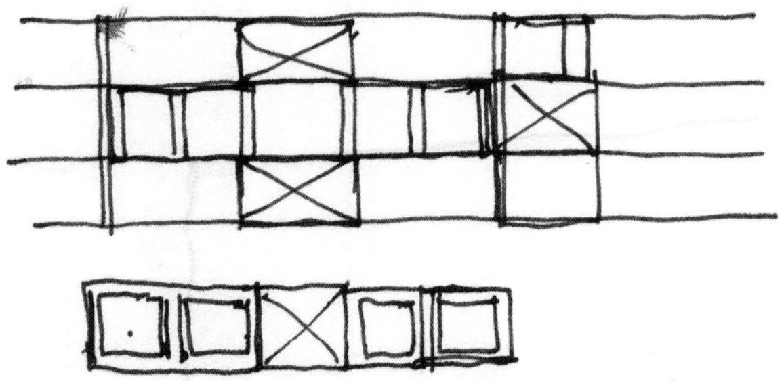

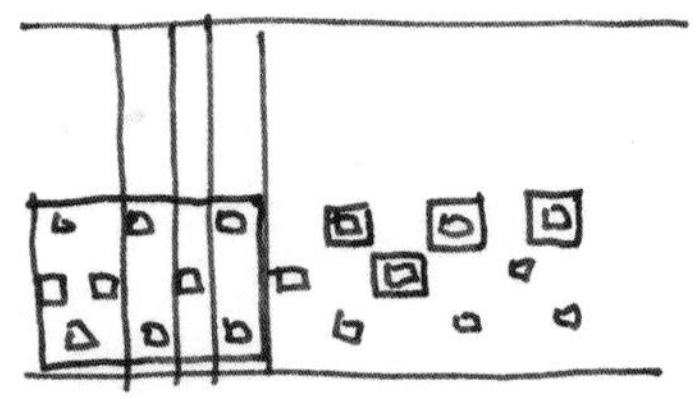

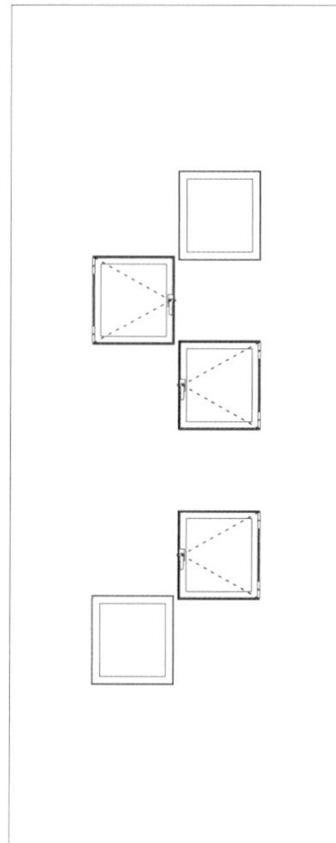

Inside

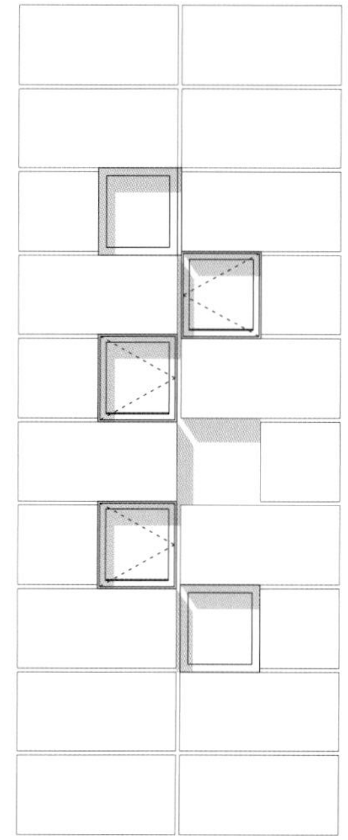

Outside

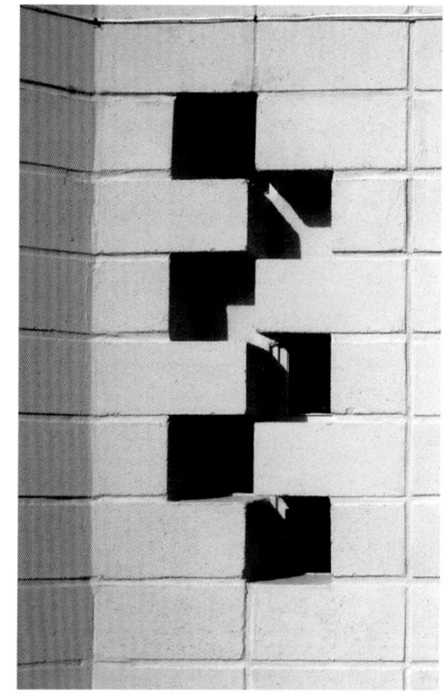

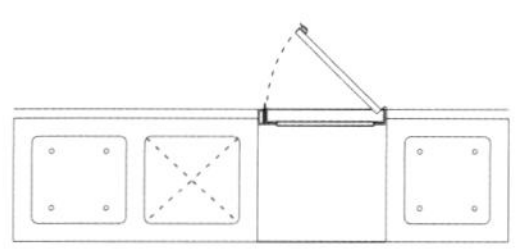

Plan

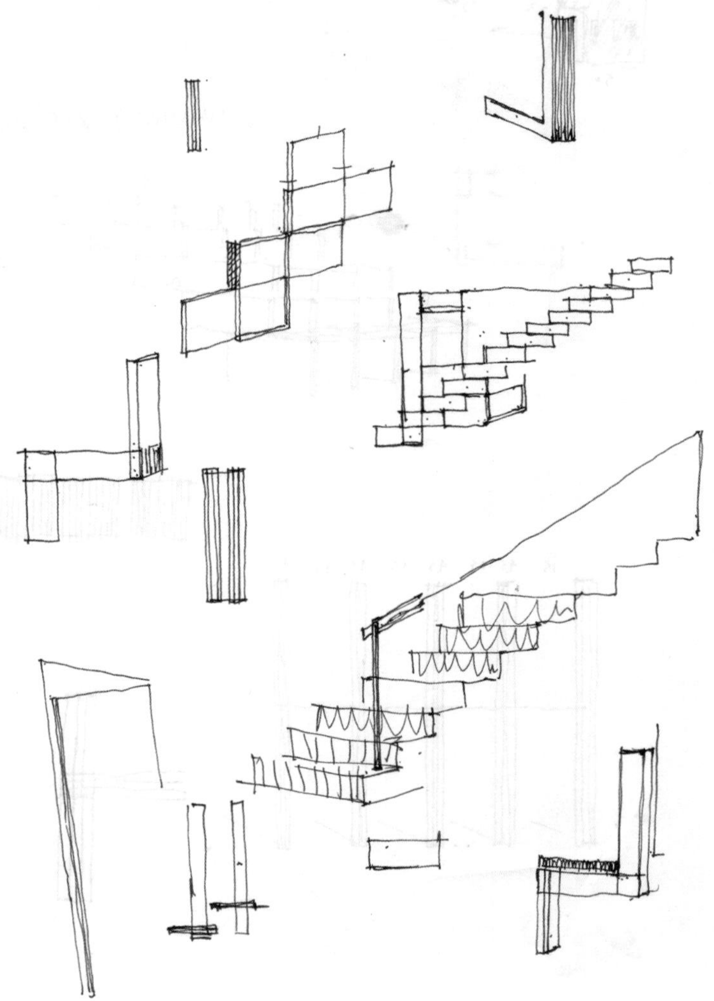

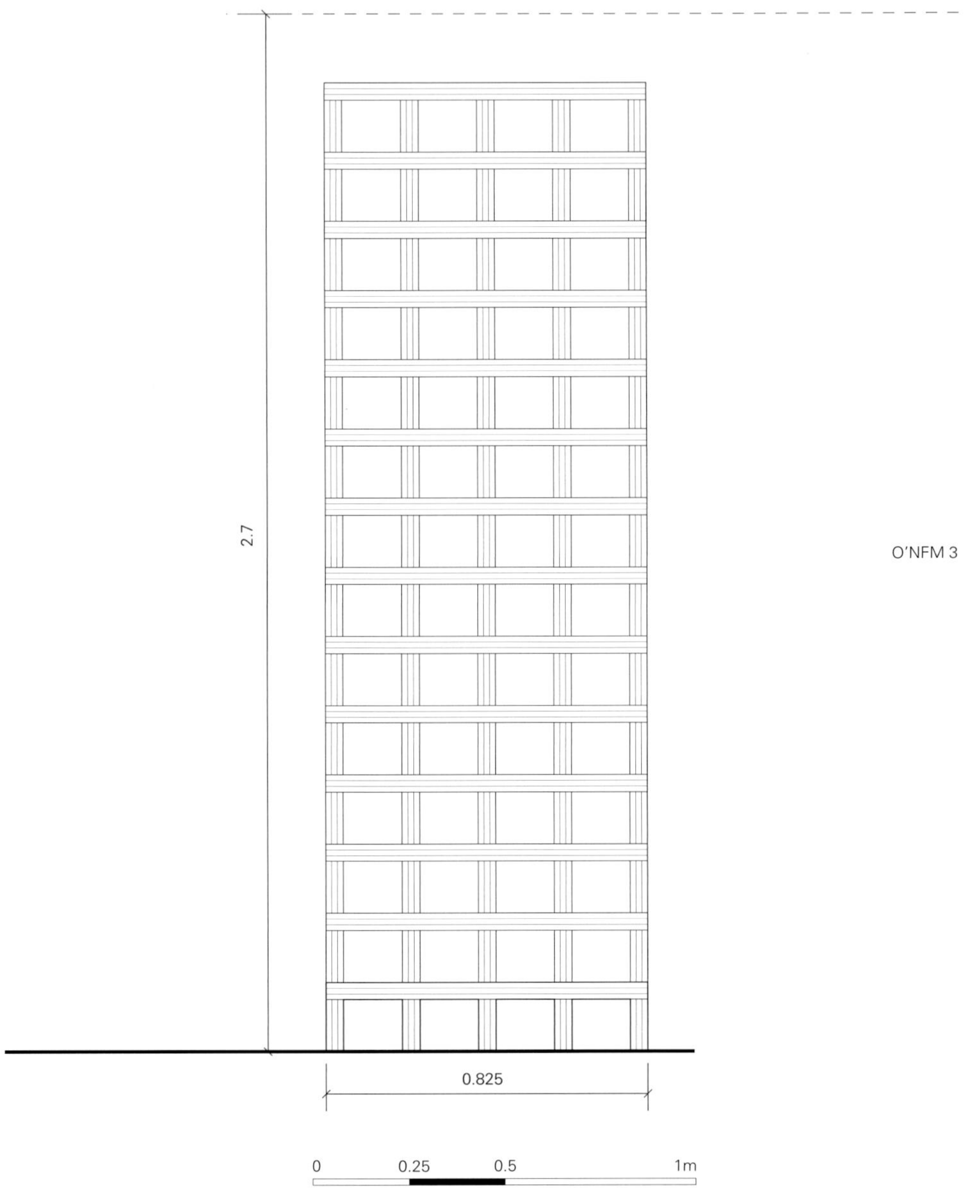

Plywood Stair Detail
Scale 1 : 20

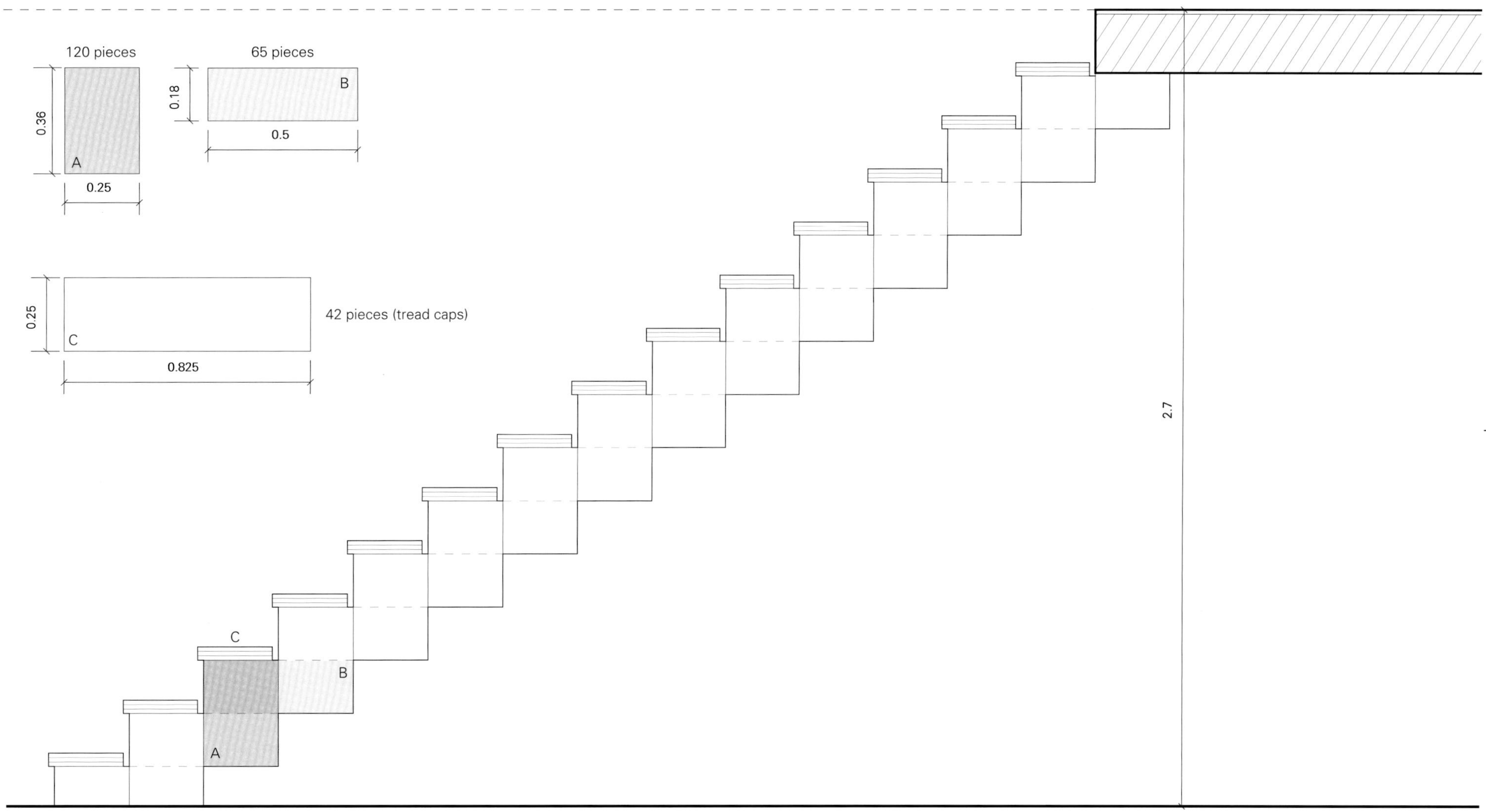
120 pieces
0.36
A
0.25
65 pieces
0.18
B
0.5
0.25
C
0.825
42 pieces (tread caps)
C
B
A
2.7

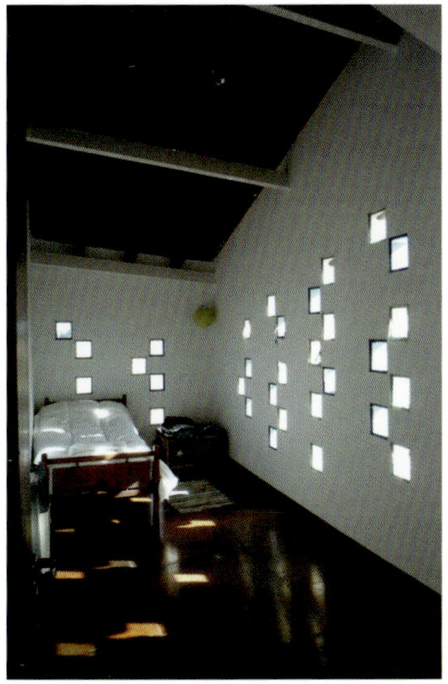

Biographies

Architects

Rafael Iglesia

Born in Concordia, Entre Rios, Argentina in 1952, Rafael Iglesia graduated in 1981 from the National University of Rosario, School of Architecture, Planning and Design. He is a founding member of the *Grupo R*, formed in 1992, and a member of the panel of judges at the Association of Architects in the Province of Santa Fe.

Iglesia is a tenured professor at the Escola de Cidade in São Paulo, Brazil. In 1991, he served as an academic advisor to the executive committee for the International Architectural Conference "The Construction of Thought." He has given taught numerous courses and lectures in Argentina and abroad, including Chile, Paraguay, Brazil, the United States of America and Spain.

His work has been honored with numerous prizes including the Cubo de Acero of the 1989 Buenos Aires International Biennale, the Silver Medal of the 1991 Buenos Aires International Biennale, second prize of the Mies van der Rohe Arquitectura Latinoamericana award of 2000, and the international prize of the XV Bienal Panamericana de Arquitectura de Quito in 2006.

Marcelo Villafañe

Born in Rosario, Argentina in 1951, Marcelo Villafañe studied architecture at the National University of Rosario from 1970–75. During this period, he also developed a passion for painting, honored with Second Prize at the Salón Nacional de Pintura de Rosario in 1983 and First Prize in 1985.

Initially, he worked for J. Bruguera Studio in Buenos Aires, Argentina before returning to Rosario in 1979 to start his own practice, which he continues with today working on both private and public commissions. He also participates in local and international design competitions, most recently receiving First Prize in the National Design Competition for the Central Coast project in Rosario. Villafañe's designs have also been featured in local and international publications.

He was a founding member of *Groupo R*, formed in 1992, and in 1998 he began working with *041 Magazine* (www.revista041.com.ar), serving as its Director since 1999. He taught at the School of Architecture at the National University of Rosario from 1996–2006 and continues to teach and lecture in South America, the United States of America and Europe.

Federico Guillermo Nicolás Pastorino

Federico Pastorino first studied under Otto Krause at the Industrial School ENET N° 1, Buenos Aires, graduating in 1997 as Maestro Mayo de Obras with honors. In 2004 he graduated as architect from the Facultad de Arquitectura, Diseño y Urbanismo, Universidad de Buenos Aires before attaining a post-graduate degree in Architecture and Technology from the Universidad Torcuato die Tella, Buenos Aires (2007). In 2011 he will recieve a Master of Architectural Design degree from the Universidad de Navarra, Pamplona.

Pastorino has also won numerous design awards including 3rd Prize in the Unipox Argentina Architectural Models Competition (2003), honorable mention for the the cultural city project student competition organized by the Central Society of Architects and Clarín (2004), honorable mention in the International Competition for a Refuge in Chan Chan, Peru, organized by Arquitectum (2006), honorable mention in the competition organized by the Banco Hipotecario for his design for social housing, and honorable mention for social housing in the competition organized by INCOSE and Clarín.

Juan Manuel Rois

Juan Manuel Rois is an Assistant Professor at the University of Illinois at Chicago.

Rois has a professional degree from the School of Architecture, Planning and Design of the National University of Rosario and a post-professional Master of Architecture from the University of Illinois at Chicago. Rois was awarded the Oberdick Fellowship from the Taubman College of Architecture and Urban Planning of The University of Michigan.

Starting his career with Marcelo Villafañe, their work together included the first prize at the National Competition for the Central Coast Area of Rosario. Besides this collaboration, Rois pursued his independent practice through various competitions, winning the first prize for the Arquitectónica Foundation Fellowship.

Currently, he maintains a Rosario-based practice, associated with Diego Arraigada. Recent awards include the second prize at the International Ideas Competition for the Metropolitan Park of the Rosario-Victoria Bridge and third prize for the National Competition for the San Fernando Riverfront.

Wilfried Wang

Wilfried Wang is the O'Neil Ford Centennial Professor in Architecture at The University of Texas at Austin. Together with Barbara Hoidn, he is founder of the office of Hoidn Wang Partner, Berlin.

Wang studied architecture in London, where he was in partnership with John Southall. In 1979 he was founding co-editor of *9H Magazine* and co-director of the 9H Gallery from 1985 to 1990. From 1995 to 2000 he was director of the German Architecture Museum.

He taught at the Polytechnic of North London, University College London, ETH Zurich, Harvard University and University of Navarra.

Wang is the author of various architectural publications. He has served on competition and award juries and is an honorary member of the Federation of German Architects, a foreign member of the Royal Swedish Academy of Arts, as well as a member of the Academy of the Arts, Berlin.

Project Credits and Information

Altamira Building

Architect	Rafael Iglesia
Collaborators	Andrés Lombardo, Mariano Fiorentini
Client	Conystar SRL
Structural Engineers	Ing. Bollero Ing. Campodónico
Construction Company	Conystar SRL
Material Supplier	Hormigón Armado
Location	470 San Luis Street Rosario, Santa Fe Argentina
Construction Area	147 m²
Total Floor Area	1,180 m²
Project Period	1998–1999
Construction Period	2000–2001

Florence Raigal House

Architect	Marcelo Villafañe
Collaborators	Laura Rois Eleonora Flores Juan Andrés Romanos
Modeling	Laura Rois Eleonora Flores Juan Andrés Romanos Fernando Brunel Florencia Faini
Constrution Supervision	Carlos Candia Marcelo Kopca
Location	Rosario Chacra Los Raigales, Roldán Argentina
Construction Area	70 m²
Lot Area	2,972 m²
Budget (U$)	$350 / m² (approx. $33 / ft²)
Project Period	2005
Construction Period	2005–2006

Selected Bibliography

Altamira Building

Editors of Phaidon Press, ed. *10x10_2: 100 Architects, 10 Critics*. London: Phaidon Press, 2005.

———. *The Phaidon Atlas of Contemporary World Architecture*. London: Phaidon Press, 2004.

Iglesia, Rafael. *AA 38, Arquitecturas de Autores / Author Architectures*. Pamplona: Universidad de Navarra, 2006.

Liernur, Jorge Francisco. "Edificio en Rosario." *Arquine: revista internacional de arquitectura*, no. 21 (Fall 2002): 38–43. In Spanish and English.

Mori, Alejandro Aravena. *Material de Arquitectura*. Edited by Alejandro Aravena Mori, Sandra Iturriaga del Campo, and Ricardo Torrejón. Serie Arquitectura-teoría y obra 5. Santiago: Ediciones Arq, 2003. In Spanish.

"Rafael Iglesia." *ARQ*, no. 51 (July 2002): 32–37. In Spanish, includes English summary.

"Rafael Iglesia: Altamira Building, Rosario, Argentina 1998–2001." *A + U: architecture and urbanism* 5, no. 464 (May 2009): 36–41. In English and Japanese.

"Rafael Iglesia: edificio Altamira, Rosario, Argentina 2001." *Casabella* 67, no. 715 (2003): 68–73. In Italian, includes English captions.

Florencia Raigal House

"Marcelo Villafañe: Florencia Raigal House, Rosario, Argentina 2005." *A + U: architecture and urbanism* 5, no. 464 (May 2009): 46–53. In English and Japanese.

Villafañe, Marcelo. "Casa en una Chacra en Roldán." In *Revista 041, Nº7*. Edited by J. Manuel Rois. Rosario: n.p., n.d. In Spanish.

———. "Casa Florencia Raigal." *Bio Revista: Arquitectura y Construción*, no. 307. In Spanish

———. *XVI Quito Pan-American Architecture Biennale Catalogue*. Quinto: BAQ, Colegio de Arquitectos del Ecuador, 2008.

Photo Credits

Cover: Cucurell Manuel and Wilfried Wang

Gustavo Farias: pages 41 (right), 43, 61 (bottom).

Gustavo Fritegotto: pages 13, 31 (right), 32, 33 (right), 36, 50 (right), 54, 56, 67, 70, 71.

Rafeal Iglesia: pages 12, 25, 27, 31 (left), 33 (left), 39, 41 (left), 61 (top), 64, 68 (right).

Cucurell Manuel: pages 8, 16, 44 (right), 45, 47) left, center), 50 (left), 51 (right), 63.

Federico Pastorino: pages 20, 29, 35, 37 (right), 44 (left), 47 (right), 48, 49, 55, 57, 60, 62, 65, 66, 68 (left), 69, 72, 73.

Walter Salcedo: pages 85, 95, 100, 101, 104, 105, 114, 115, 117 (right), 118, 119 (right), 120 (right), 121, 122, 123 (right, bottom), 124 (bottom), 125, 126 (top, right), 129 (right), 131 (left), 132, 133, 134, 135, 136, 137, 138.

Marcelo Villafañe: 116, 117 (top), 123 (top), 124 (top left, right), 139.

Wilfried Wang: pages 14, 24 (right), 37 (left), 38, 40, 42, 46, 79, 80, 109, 117 (bottom), 119 (left), 120, 126 (bottom), 127, 128, 129 (left), 130, 131 (right).